A Tail of Three Cavachons

The Turd Head Trio

So .... Who Rescued Who?

Written by "The Boys' Mum"

Disclaimer:
These stories are based on true events, involving the authors real friends and dogs. While some events have been lightly adapted or exaggerated for storytelling purposes, all names and core experiences remain true to life. This book is a celebration of real-life mischief, love, chaos, and companionship.

*To **Lexie** - who sees the world in her own beautiful way. For being the incredible, resilient, kind-hearted soul at the heart of it all. You have taught me more than I could ever teach you. You are brave, brilliant, and utterly you. Never change.*

*To **"Dad"** - who never asked for this much fur but stayed anyway. For putting up with every muddy paw print, chewed sock, shredded tea towel, and "surprise" animal I have brought into what was once a calm, quiet life. Thank you for loving me for exactly who I am and for loving our boys and our cats, even when the house is in disarray, and you are sat on a coffee table with a cushion instead of a chair.*

*To **Bill, Bailey, Teddy, Autumn, and Winter** - the paws who walk beside us. Thank you for the endless laughs, cuddles, and the kind of unconditional love that only comes with fur and floppy ears. You have filled our lives with joy, noise, and biscuit crumbs.*

*To **our fur-family friends** - the beautiful, bonkers community we found through our Cavachon journey. You have been there for the walks, the storms, the shenanigans, the cake, and everything in between. I would not be without you now.*

*And to **Ted and Summer** - the wise old souls who walked beside us until it was time to rest. You are still with us, in every wag, every meow, and every heart. We carry you with us, always.*

FOREWORD.

They say life rarely goes to plan. Ours was no exception. But somewhere between the chewed socks, stolen sandwiches, public humiliation and the comforting weight of a dog's head on a tear-soaked lap, we found something better than any plan could have offered. We found love, loyalty, laughter, and a bit of mayhem.

This book is not just about dogs, though they are, without question, the stars. It is about what happens when you open your heart to a scruffy-faced pup with a mischievous glint in his eye. Then another. Then… well, let's just say we stopped counting the socks and started counting the stories.

It began with Ted. A gentle soul who healed our hearts at a time when grief had left us lost. He led the way. Patiently showing us that it is okay to feel everything. To sit still with sadness, and to wag your tail at joy when it finally returns.

Then came Bill. Who never got the "good boy" memo. Full of spirit and uproar. He turned the quiet into adventure and taught us that not all heroes sit when told. With Bill, life got louder, messier, and far more magical.

And just when we thought our hearts were full. Bailey and Teddy arrived. Two rescue boys, full of quirks and stories of their own. Who fit into our lives like they had always been there. Together, these three formed the Turd Head Trio. A name born in jest but now worn with pride.

This is a book about dogs, but it is also about family, friendship, grief, hope, neurodiversity, healing, community, unconditional love. And the utter, glorious madness of being a dog mum.

So, whether you are a fellow dog-lover, a weary parent, or just someone who has ever been licked at an inconvenient moment. This book is for you.

Hold on tight. There will be laughter. There may be tears. And at least one chapter involving mayhem.

Welcome to our story.

The Boys' Mum

First Meeting – Bill and Ted

It started with a tumble.

From the moment Bill bounded into the room, it was clear he had no idea what "calm" meant. With puppy energy pouring out of every pore and paw, Bill immediately zoned in on Ted. The older dog, as the perfect playmate. Bill, eight weeks old, a Cavachon, with amazing eyebrows, fluffy as a dandelion and just as wild. Charged into the house like a caffeinated teddy bear on roller skates. He was all paws, no brakes, ears too big for his head, and a bark that sounded more like a squeaky toy than an actual threat.

And there, in the living room, settled like the king he was, the family dog. Beautiful, peaceful, gracious Ted. Up until this point Ted had been an only dog.

When Lexie, (Teds human sister) arrived home she was just 8 months old. Crawling, crying, curious, and oh so messy. She did not understand this new world she had entered. But Ted suddenly knew that this tiny person was his. To watch, to guide, to protect. Ted watched Lexie like a gentle guardian. When she cried, he looked curiously, head cocked to the side as if to say, "What can I do to help?". When she crawled, Ted commando crawled behind her. Ted was the first one to make Lexie laugh, really laugh, from that moment on, Ted was more than just a dog. He had helped Mum and Dad through one of the darkest, most painful times in their lives.

He had helped Mum from that darkness, into the light and out into the world again. Ted had done the same for Lexie. Once upon a time, taking a baby girl under his paw and changing all their lives forever.

Here he was now, one wise old dog, elder statesman of the household. A tricolour Cavalier King Charles Spaniel with a calm soul, wise eyes, and the permanent air of someone who had been through it all and didn't care for nonsense. Sitting with a look somewhere between bewildered and mildly horrified. He gave Bill the slowest, most sceptical blink imaginable, as if silently asking, "Who invited this whirlwind of chaos?" Bill, oblivious to the silent judgment, bounced closer, tail wagging like a tiny flag in a storm, ready to pounce.

They locked eyes. Bill let out an excited yap. Ted blinked slowly.

Bill bounced forward, tail wagging, nose sniffing, full of excitement and zero spatial awareness.

Ted raised one regal eyebrow and took a step back.

Bill launched into full zoomies within ten seconds. He ran in circles, tried to play-bow but accidentally somersaulted into the settee, chased his tail then tried to chase Ted's tail.

Ted sighed, not dramatically, just enough to make his opinion known. Lexie giggled.

Bill tried everything. Play-fighting with Ted's ears, barking directly into his face, bringing him an old sock (a peace offering?) rolling over and showing his tummy, while still kicking Ted in the face.

Ted endured it all, with the patience of a saint or perhaps a dog who knew escape was impossible.

Eventually, Ted hopped onto the settee, his throne, where "the puppy" could not reach him.

Bill tried anyway and failed. Twice.

Then something happened. Something magical. Bill, finally tired, flopped on the floor beneath the settee.

He let out a huff. Ted peeked over the edge. The tiny pup's head rested on his own paw.

His eyes fluttered shut. He gave the softest little sigh. Ted blinked again. SILENCE.

Then, without a sound, he climbed down, circled once, and lay beside him. Not close. But close enough.

And there, the two of them napped for the first time. The elder and the chaos.

The calm and the storm.

Ted's Quiet Decision

Ted was not impressed. Not with the squeaks. Not with the zoomies. Not with the sock theft. And certainly not with the puddle Bill had left by the rabbit hutch where the house rabbit, aptly named by Lexie "Bunny" resided.

Ted watched the tiny puppy, who had now been in his house for exactly six days, tumble headfirst into a dog bed, dragging a slipper with him like a trophy.

Bill snored almost instantly. Ted blinked. It wasn't that Ted disliked him. Bill was just… too much. Too loud. Too fast. Too sticky.

And yet, something had changed.

Bill had stopped trying so hard to impress him.

He no longer barked directly into Ted's face or attempted mid-air tackles. Instead, he just followed. Not closely. Not intrusively. But enough that Ted always knew where he was.

That night, the house fell quiet. Lexie was tucked in. Mum and Dad had collapsed on the settee, and Ted, padding into the hallway to check everything was in its place, found Bill curled into a fluffy ball on the rug, tail twitching in a dream. He looked smaller when he was still. Softer. Lonelier. Ted stood there a moment. Then slowly, deliberately, he lowered himself beside the pup. Close enough to touch. Bill shifted. Snuggled closer.

Still asleep but now smiling. Ted sighed, resting his chin across Bill's back. Bill let out a contented breath, pressed against him like he had always belonged there. That was the first night they slept together. No fuss. No drama. Just quiet understanding. Bill had found his safe place. Right there curled under the chin of the gentlest, kindest big brother in the world.

From that moment on, they were never apart for long. Ted taught Bill how to bark at the postman properly. Ted even barked when Bill needed to go out to the toilet.

Bill taught Ted how to move faster rather than having a nap every hour.

Ted showed Bill the best spots to lie in the sun.

Bill showed Ted how to ruin those spots by digging holes in the garden.

They were not the same. They did not always understand each other, but they were brothers from day one. And Ted? He never quite admitted it, but deep down, he liked the noise. He learnt to love the little chaotic whirlwind that had entered his life in the form of Bill. Even when it came with chewed slippers.

This was the start of something special, incredibly special. It was the beginning of a lifelong friendship, full of mischief, surprises, and, mostly, patience.

The First Play.

Ted did not play. He was too grown up. Too wise. Too dignified.

Ted preferred sunbathing, people-watching, and the occasional slow trot through the garden. He had seen toys, of course. Chewed a few in his younger years. But these days, fun was for pups.

Enter Bill.

Bill thought everything was a game. A stick? Game. Mum's slipper? Game. A leaf blowing across the floor? Game of the century. Ted ignored him, mostly. Bill would bounce around him with a ball, wagging like a wind-up toy, begging, "Chase me! Tug this! Play with me!". Ted would lift an eyebrow, turn away, go back to his corner of the rug like a royal snubbing a jester, until one afternoon. Bill had been particularly insistent. He paraded around with yet another new toy, a soft toy that squeaked; a pink bedraggled hippo that already looked like a crime scene. Ted huffed. Bill squeaked. Ted blinked. Bill squeaked again.

And again. And then Ted stood up. Bill froze.

Was this it? Was he in trouble? Was the older dog finally going to tell him off?

Ted took one slow, deliberate step forward. Then another. And then, pounced.

Not fast. Not fierce. But very much a pounce. He grabbed Mr. Squeaks with a deep, rumbling growl of pretend drama and gave it a half-hearted shake.

Bill yapped with joy. Lexie sat on the sofa watching and laughing.

He leapt back into the game, growling playfully, tail whirling, eyes wide with the thrill of being seen, really seen, by his hero.

For ten whole minutes, Ted played. He let Bill tug. He chased him, very slowly at first. He barked, he, too, wagged his tail. He even seemed to smile. And when they finally collapsed onto the floor, panting and grinning, Bill tucked himself into the crook of Ted's belly like a puzzle piece sliding into place. Mum snapped a photo. Lexie whispered, "They're best friends now." And they were.

Ted's Failed Masterclass: How to Be a Good Boy

Ted had always been the model citizen of the house. Calm, patient, and never one to shred a cushion just for fun. Naturally, Mum assumed he would be the perfect mentor to show Bill the ropes. Mum was wrong.

On their first day in matching sweaters, Ted tried to set an example, sitting stoically on the settee, eyes front, behaving impeccably. Ted, the elder statesman. Dignified, calm, partial to a walk, a snooze, and a carrot. He had long since earned his spot on the settee and the right to judge others from it.

Then came Bill. Bill could not sit still for two seconds. He bounced from cushion to cushion like a furry pinball, nearly toppling over Ted in his excitement. He chewed everything. He barked at shadows, he tried to eat his own tail. He once got stuck behind the settee, trying to retrieve a sock.

Then there was the time Ted, ever the gentleman, watched Bill steal a bright yellow bra from the laundry pile and parade it around the house like a prize-winning trophy. Ted sighed deeply, as if to say, "This is not how it's done."

And let's not forget the shredded paper incident. Ted, perfectly nestled in his bed, looked on in horror as Bill tore through a pile of wrapping paper like a wild raccoon, leaving a trail of havoc in his wake.

Ted showed Bill how to greet people politely. Bill would leap at them, licking, wriggling, knocking glasses off noses.

Ted would lie gracefully on the rug. Bill would lie on Ted. Ted would wait calmy at the door. Bill would bolt past it.

What Bill would do, was let Lexie cry tears into his fur without barking mid-hug. After all Lexie hated hugs, except from Bill and Ted.

Ted would watch, give him a slow blink, a quiet nod. As if to say, "You're not quite a good boy yet, but you're getting there."

Bill would wag his tail so hard it thumped like a drum. And, for just that moment, Bill was everything Ted hoped he would be… until he peed on the carpet.

When Bill got too much, and he often did, Ted would give him "The Look." Not aggressive. Not angry, just disappointed. A look that said, "You are making us both look bad!"

Despite Ted's best efforts, Bill's idea of "being a good boy" remained blissfully and mischievously his own.

Bill's Life of Crime (and His Feline Accomplice)

Walks were never simple with Bill. While Ted stayed politely by Mums side, Bill would vanish into the undergrowth like a furry ninja, always on a mission of his own. No matter how peaceful the woods looked, Bill would return with twigs in his beard, a cheeky glint in his eye, and absolutely no regrets.

Things got even more chaotic when Autumn, the family cat, joined the rebellion.

It started innocently. A shared water bowl here, a sniff there. But before long, Autumn was hopping onto counters, scouting snacks, while Bill waited below like a tiny, bearded getaway driver. If something mysteriously went missing from the kitchen counter, you could bet it was a two-species operation.

Inside the house, Bill's hobbies included: destroying packaging with glee, turning pillows into snowstorms, and most impressively hollowing out a tennis ball and stuffing it full of kibble like a homemade vending machine. Creativity and bedlam in equal measure.

Ted, the long-suffering elder, simply watched on. Eyes full of weary wisdom, as Bill continued his reign of mischief with gusto, and now he had backup.

By the time Bill hit his teenage months, he had truly embraced his role as household hooligan. He had perfected his "innocent eyes" act, usually deployed seconds after some act of sabotage. But the day of the biscuit heist? That was Bill at his most brilliant... and most devious. It began with a suspicious silence. Always a bad sign.

Upon entering the kitchen, Mum found Autumn perched nonchalantly on the worktop, directly beside an open container of biscuits. Below, Bill sat perfectly still, crumbs dusting his muzzle like a beard of guilt, and one broken biscuit still clutched gently in his paws like a trophy.

There were no signs of struggle, just the quiet aftermath of a well-executed mission. Judging by the suspicious teamwork and the trail of pawprints. Mum suspected that Autumn knocked the lid loose... and Bill handled the "retrieval."

Ted, wisely, stayed far away.

From that day on, Mum never underestimated the power of teamwork, especially when one of the team members had claws and the other had a criminal mind.

From then on Bill and Autumn were unstoppable. Mum soon learnt not to leave food out "defrosting" Bill and Autumn did not understand what "defrosting meant."

Mum had left two plump chicken breasts, neatly wrapped in cling film, "defrosting" on the kitchen worktop alongside some jacket potatoes all ready for the air fryer later. Salad prepped, feeling, for once, like a proper organised grown-up. "Right," she said, sliding on her coat and grabbing the keys. "Lex, let's go. Twenty minutes, in and out." She turned to Bill, already lounging under the table with his paws crossed like he ran the place. Ted quietly snoring in his bed. "No counter surfing. I mean it." Bill didn't move. Just blinked. Slowly. Innocently. Autumn the cat, curled like a coiled spring on the windowsill, gave no such reassurances. He opened one eye, yawned like a lion, and stretched.

Mum should have known. She did know. But she left anyway.

The second the front door clicked shut, game mode activated.

Autumn, sleek and efficient, slinked down from his perch, he took a moment to survey the scene: one bowl of potatoes, two chicken breasts, and one overexcited dog practically vibrating with anticipation below him. Bill whined softly. Just once.

Autumn didn't even glance at him. He was already leaping onto the worktop like a graceful burglar, tail swishing as he examined his options. He started with a potato. A light nudge. It rolled dramatically across the worktop, hovered for a moment at the edge, then plummeted to the floor with a dull thud.

Bill pounced, inhaled it, chewed twice, then decided it was boring and spat it out.

Autumn glared at him, "Focus!" he seemed to say. Then - the chicken. With surgical precision, he pawed one of the cling-film-wrapped breasts to the edge. It slid… paused… and tumbled.

Bill caught it mid-air like a golden retriever in a dog food commercial. Gone in seconds. He looked up, amazed. Autumn was a God.

Autumn sent the second chicken breast flying, then launched a second potato for fun. By the time Mum's car rolled back onto the drive, Autumn was back on the windowsill cleaning his ears like he had spent the afternoon meditating and Bill was sprawled belly-up on the floor, full to bursting.

The moment Mum walked in, she knew. The silence. The crumbs. The single potato slowly rolling across the tiles like a scene from a crime documentary. "Oh, Bill," Mum groaned. "Not again." He didn't move. Just wagged his tail once.

Autumn didn't even blink. Lexie stepped in behind her, sniffed the air, and frowned.

Mum pointed at Bill. "We had chicken!"

Lexie turned to Autumn. "Autumn?"

Autumn yawned, looked straight through her, and tucked a paw under his chest with a purr. That night, they had baked beans on toast. Again

The next morning, Mum printed a sign in bold black letters:

"THE COUNTER IS NOT A BUFFET."

She taped it to the fridge. And the cupboard. And the oven. Bill sniffed each one thoughtfully. Autumn knocked the fridge sign off with one gentle flick of his paw.

And still, it wasn't the end. Because once the heist had happened once, the thrill was there. Bill now hovered hopefully under every worktop. Autumn took to rattling the cupboard doors when he was bored. Dear Ted just sat and watched it all unfold. He had given up trying to give his little brother any advice at all.

One week later, Mum left out sausages defrosting. Another rookie mistake. She returned to find the tray completely empty and Autumn sitting smugly in the middle of the counter licking the condensation off the window like it was wine. Bill, bloated and satisfied, was asleep inside Ted's basket. Ted looked up at if to say, "Sorry mum, I'm done trying"

A new note appeared the next day: Presumably from Dad.

"THIS IS WHY WE CAN'T HAVE NICE THINGS."

Autumn knocked that one down too.

Bill's Big Misadventures: The Mayhem Maestro

As Bill grew, so did his talent for destruction. No pillow, slipper, remote control, or laundry pile was safe. His favourite trick? Waiting until the house was just quiet enough, then launching into an unsupervised art project, typically involving something soft or expensive:

- Lexie's headphones: 0 - Bill 3
- Lexie's school bag and its contents: 0 - Bill 2
- Lexie's homework: 0 - Bill 1
- Lexie's glasses 0 - Bill 4 (+ phone call to vet's)
- Dad's new work boots: 0 - Bill 1
- Dad's lunch bag: 0 - Bill 2
- Mum's purse and contents: 0 - Bill 3
- Mum's handbag and contents: 0 - Bill 2
- Ted's medication box: 0 - Bill 1 (+ trip to vet's and bill)

Mum sought advice. She booked a session with a behaviourist, a proper one, qualified, calm, clipboard, everything. Mum explained it all, the theft, the destruction, the dog, and cat duo.

The behaviourist listened quietly. Took notes, watched Bill chewing on a toy like it owed him money. Then looked at Mum, smiled and said gently, "He's just very intelligent!"

Lexie laughed. Mum blinked, "Sorry what, but he's SO naughty."

The behaviourist explained "He's not being naughty he's entertaining himself."

Mum stared at Bill who was now trying to get into the behaviourist's bag to see what he could get out of there. "Right" Mum said, "so I've got a genius."

"Yes" the behaviourist nodded, "and a bored one."

Mum had a new understanding Bill was not naughty he was BRILLIANT, A GENIUS. Lexie knew it.

Mum told Dad "Bill's a GENIUS! The behaviourist said so himself."

Dad rolled his eyes and said "Ok" quietly looking at Ted and whispered, "oh dear God!"

From that day on Mum tried EVERYTHING, enrichment puzzles, jobs, challenges, but Bill declined them all, instead of engaging, he again destroyed them all and more.

Mum once returned to find what looked like snow covering the kitchen floor. It wasn't snow. It was a brand-new bag of cat litter, three cushions, and a festive pillow that would never see another Christmas.

Ted stood at a safe distance, watching like a weary crime scene witness.

Bill didn't stop there he continued. Chewed up shoes? Check. Deconstructed squeaky toys? Check. Ripped magazines, half-eaten cardboard, stolen washing… double check. He even found joy in reorganizing dirty clothes. Often while perched proudly in the middle of the pile with the cat nearby, clearly approving. He was chaos with eyebrows. A one-dog demolition squad with a beard. And somehow, despite it all, completely irresistible.

Mum repeatedly told Dad, "He's not bad, he's just clever, a GENIUS" Bill, brilliant, bold, and always one paw ahead.

The Art of Pretending: Bill Goes Legit (Sort Of)

Somewhere between chewed slippers and a destroyed remote, Mum decided Bill might benefit from some structure. So off he went to training classes where, to Dad's surprise, he thrived.

He sat. He stayed. He high fived. He even earned rosettes and certificates. To onlookers, he was the image of a reformed rogue.

But Mum knew the truth: Bill had learned how to pretend.

Behind the scenes, uproar still reigned. The moment Bill got home, it was business as usual. Muddy paws, ripped post, and mysterious objects relocated to his secret stash behind the settee. At training, He met new doggy friends, Bobby, and Bunty, the three of them together ran with the kind of wild energy that could strip paint off a fence. They were his partners in early chaos, his puppyhood partners-in-crime.

Even his human sister Lexie gave him "the talk" - paws in hands, a serious face-to-snout chat about behaviour. Bill nodded solemnly, blinking like he understood every word. And then, within minutes, he was wrestling a tea towel like he really wanted to dry the dishes.

His obedience was real… but selective. He was learning. But mostly, he was learning how to get away with it.

Bobby, yes, he is a boy, a fellow Cavachon, sweet-faced but just as naughty as Bill; and Bunty, a shameless Bedlington Terrier flirt, who could charm the sausage out of any trainer's pocket. There on their training field these three misfits fell in love. And Bill, Bobby and Bunty's mums formed an eternal understanding and friendship. Supposed to be a place of structure and obedience. It was… not.

But the three of them together, Bill, Bobby and Bunty decided they wanted to teach each other rather than listen to the instructor. While the other pups sat politely, Bill would roll onto his back mid-class, paws in the air like he had decided training was optional. Bobby followed suit, barking with delight. Bunty sashayed across the field like she owned it. And the mums? Well, they were no better.

There was a lot of laughter. A lot of whispering. A lot of, "Oh no, not those three again." Bill was never sure if they were talking about them or the "Mums."

Mum had made new friends. Mum looked forward to her weekly catch up of how awful or slightly good Bill had been that week, stories of Bobby and Bunty made them all laugh, sometimes cry, but the best thing about it was the dogs had fun and so did the mums.

Each week felt like a therapy session, for the Mums. The trainers were not impressed though with either the dogs or the Mums. The frenzy escalated. Bill was pulling, Bobby was bouncing, Bunty was doing her usual flirt and frolic with every dog within a six-foot radius. The Mums they were talking, too much, apparently.

"Bunty's Mum!" the instructor snapped "Are you listening?" The whole class went quiet. Bunty's mum, who had been talking but also trying her best with a bag of treats looked up and froze. "I - I'm sorry" she stammered.

The instructor rolled his eyes "Do you even want to be here? It's not good enough."

That's when it happened. Bunty's mum sank slowly to the ground, right there in the middle of the field, and cried.

Bill's Mum stood still. Dead still. Something inside her ignited, fierce, maternal, protective. "We are trying our best!" she shouted.

The instructor laughed, actually laughed, then muttered something under his breath.

That was it, Bills mum launched Bills water bottle, not at the instructor but in his general direction, turned on her heel, bursting into angry frustrated tears as she stormed away from the class and the rest of the training group. Behind her Bunty's Mum, teary eyed and grateful. Bobby's Mum, fuming with solidarity but most surprising of all, Bill, Bobby and Bunty trotting behind their Mum's, ears down and clearly just as upset.

From the sidelines came the muttering. "Oh God, here they go again, are we ever going to learn anything in these classes or are we just here for their drama?"

The Mums turned, glared, held each other's eyes, then burst out laughing, through the tears, the shouting, the pandemonium, they had found something stronger than a training technique. FRIENDSHIP. And the dogs? They covered their Mums in muddy, stinky licks, fully endorsing the mutiny.

They never went back to that class. Instead, they did something better: walks, gossip, pub lunches. Training - not so much, but love, support, laughter - every single week. From that day on, everyone knew, those three Mums, those three dogs - they were a pack. Unbreakable.

The Heart Beneath the Havoc

For all his wild outbursts and shredded surprises, Bill's heart was never in doubt.

As Ted grew older and began to slow down, Bill, the same dog who once treated Ted like a trampoline, became gentle. He would curl beside him instead of on top, nudge his brother awake with the softest nose bop, and stayed close when Ted needed rest. Mischief paused for love.

But it was with his human sister Lexie that Bill's deepest loyalty shone. When she was happy, he would bounce with her. When she was tired, he would lie still, head on her chest, as if guarding her heartbeat. He seemed to know when she needed him most - no words necessary.

Sure, the cardboard might still mysteriously explode. And no slipper could ever feel safe. But these were just quirks of a dog whose love ran wild and deep.

Bill was mischief wrapped in fluff, trouble on four legs, but also the heartbeat of our home. A best friend. A furry sibling. A companion through every storm and occasionally, the cause of one.

Sometimes, Bill seemed to carry two personalities inside his fluffy little frame: one was the soft, soulful side that snuggled up to Lexie after a long day, gently resting his head on her lap like he was anchoring her to the earth and the other was the whirlwind who had just ten minutes earlier reduced a cardboard box to rubble and hidden one of your socks inside a shoe.

He could go from cuddles to carnage and back again in the blink of an eye.

But there were moments that made Mum and Dad pause, when Ted was poorly and Bill never left his side, not even for treats. When Lexie had a hard day and Bill climbed into her arms without a single cue. When he rested his paw on her knee like a tiny furry therapist who didn't charge a fee (except maybe in biscuits).

Despite everything he chewed, dragged, or dismantled, Bill never once damaged something truly important. He knew where the heart of the home was, and he made sure we always knew it too.

He was not perfect, but he was perfect for them.

Rain or shine, Bill was there, usually in a muddy raincoat, often up to no good.

Holidays with Bill were an adventure in themselves. He didn't care if it poured, if the caravan was small, or if his paws were caked in muck. Every outing was a new chance to dash off, dig something, or defy all training. And he always returned as if to say, "Wasn't that the best day ever?" Even when he looked like a swamp creature, or when he was dressed, begrudgingly (along with Dear Ted) as a dinosaur, Bill remained utterly, unshakably himself.

He shared everything with Lexie, the car rides, the lazy afternoons, the quiet support during tough moments. You could always find them wrapped up together, her hand on his paw, his head nestled into her side. There were times it seemed like they didn't need words just each other.

And through it all, Ted was never far. Steady, wise, and increasingly tolerant, he watched Bill with that quiet "Oh no, not again" expression that only an older sibling can truly master. The three of them, Lexie, Ted, and Bill formed a bond stronger than rules, furniture, or torn paper could ever break.

In every muddy pawprint and every chewed toy, in every ruined slipper and belly laugh, Bill left his mark. And while the madness still rolls in waves, one truth remains steady:

He was joy in a fur coat.

Sandy Paws and Seaside Adventures

Heading off on their summer holiday to their favourite beach at Perranporth. None of them knew it would be Ted's last holiday with them, not even him. If he did, he kept it to himself, choosing instead to soak up every moment like the wise old soul he was.

The car was chaos, dogs everywhere, bags packed into every corner, Lexie squashed between Bill and Ted with her knees under her chin and a bag of snacks balanced on her lap. Mum shouted out the car window, to Dad still heaving things out the house "Have we got the dog bowls, their beds, food, toys, treats, balls?!"

Dad, already done with the day, muttered, "We're not even left yet."

When they finally reached Perranporth, Ted did what he always did. He stepped out of the car, sniffed the salty sea air, then gave Bill the look that quiet look that said, "Go on then, off you go," as if passing the baton of beach mischief. And Bill did. Like a cannonball of mayhem, he launched into the dunes, barking at the wind, digging holes he had no intention of filling back in.

Ted followed slower, more measured, but still with that same glint in his eye.

Bill, still unsure about waves, charged at them like a tiny lifeguard on duty, then immediately ran the other way.

Ted, wise and calm, found the comfiest towel spot and refused to budge.

They played mini golf, well, the humans did, whilst Bill tried to steal the balls, made new animal friends at a local farm, and discovered that chips always taste better outdoors. The caravan park became their temporary kingdom, where Lexie, Bill and Ted snuggled under the covers at night, sharing dreams of the day's mischief.

Bill had grown used to the idea that family fun didn't always mean being dry, clean, or well-behaved. Rainy days didn't stop them, not when there were steam trains to ride and window seats to squish into with his brother Ted and his human sister, his best friend. Bill loved the train's steady rhythm, but most of all, he loved the curious looks from fellow passengers who were not used to two wet, mucky dogs enjoying the ride as much as any human.

In the car, Ted and now Bill made their throne of blankets, helped by Lexie, perched in regal comfort as the family travelled from one countryside adventure to the next. He ruled the back seat with sandy paws and a slightly suspicious stare, always ready to leap into action… or nap, depending on the snacks available.

No matter how many miles they travelled or memories they made, one thing stayed the same, Bill's flair for mischief. Even when out and about, Bill could not resist adding drama to an otherwise peaceful walk. He was fast, he was loud, and he was always just one step away from his next caper.

That week was magic. Ted didn't run like he used to, but he still pottered through the rock pools, climbed halfway up the dunes, before waiting to be put in the beach cart to be pulled up cardiac hill by Dad. He barked at seagulls just for the sport of it. Bill tried to herd the tide. Lexie giggled with laughter as the boys chased after her, splashing in and out of the waves like wild things.

Every evening, after a long day of sunshine, sea air and sandy snacks, Ted would curl beside Bill in the caravan, both snoring in harmony while Dad did a BBQ and Mum sat with her book.

There were moments on that trip, small, fleeting ones, that in hindsight feel heavier. Ted lingering at the top of the hill overlooking the sea, just watching. Ted letting Bill steal the ball without protest. Ted sleeping more deeply, snuggling more gently. Mum didn't say anything. Mum did not know. But maybe Ted did.

On the final morning, Mum and Lexie walked down to the beach early. Just them. The sky soft and grey, the tide halfway in. Ted sat facing the sea. Bill lay beside him, head resting across Ted's back. Lexie stood in silence, holding both boys' leads. And Mum stood a few steps back, not daring to interrupt what felt like a goodbye wrapped in peace. Mum took a hundred photos. She just didn't know they would be the last of them all together on "Ted's beach." But what a last they were.

Slowing Down but Never Apart

Bill had been with the family for almost two years. Ted was no longer the sprightly pup he once was. His pace slowed, his naps grew longer, and stairs became more of a mountain than a molehill. His eyes now carried a gentle tiredness, but they still twinkled whenever he saw Lexie and Bill or smelt something delicious.

Bill noticed. At first, he did not understand why Ted was not joining in the madness anymore. He would nudge him, bark at him, even try dragging him into games. But slowly, Bill changed too. He sat beside Ted more. Waited for him. Protected him. And when Ted did not want to be alone, Bill curled up close, offering the warmth and comfort only a brother could give.

On walks, Bill would pause and look back if Ted was too far behind. If Ted stopped altogether, Bill would sit down, refusing to move without him. Lexie would watch and wait too; the "Three musketeers" side by side.

Inside the house, things were quieter. Ted rested often, but never far from the family. And Bill? He never let Ted feel forgotten. He brought him toys, even chewed ones, licked his ears, and sometimes just lay nearby, watching.

Over the weeks, something shifted. Ted slowed down. And Bill, just a little, started watching him more. Started mirroring him. Started trying.

He still messed up. He still howled randomly, tore around the garden like a lunatic, and once peed on Ted, Mum liked to think it was accidental... she hoped. But he also cuddled up next to his big brother, followed him on walks, and shared his carrots with him.

And Ted? Ted softened.

Maybe he knew his time was changing. That this tornado of a pup was his legacy. Maybe he realised he couldn't teach Bill to be perfect, but he could teach him to be loyal, to be gentle with Lexie, to show up when someone needed him. And that mattered more than being a "good boy" all the time.

That last holiday together, Ted watched Bill gallop across the sand, like a dog-shaped kite, tripping over his own paws, barking at the wind. Ted didn't join him; he just lay quietly on the beach, eyes following every bounce, every bark, every bit of ridiculous joy.

And for the first time, Ted didn't look disappointed. He looked proud.

Because he hadn't raised a perfect pup. He had raised Bill.

Bill might still be wild, messy, and unpredictable but when it came to Ted, he was gentle, loyal, loving. And that mattered more than any rosette or training class ever could.

A Gentle Goodbye

The family began to notice. Ted didn't bark as much at the Ring doorbell. He needed help up to the sofa. Mum, obviously, bought him his own settee steps. His tail wagged slower, but it still wagged. He never stopped loving, but his body had grown tired.

Lexie sat beside him more. Sometimes with her iPad sharing a film, sometimes in silence. She would stroke his fur and whisper stories. Bill lay on the other side, resting his chin on Ted's back like a guard who wouldn't leave his post.

Bill didn't cause havoc those days. He stayed close. He watched Lexie's face, sensed her sadness. He didn't understand everything, but he knew, Ted wasn't quite the same.

Ted had given them everything; his loyalty, his laughter, his patience, his love. Helped Mum and Dad through one of the darkest and saddest times of their lives when he first arrived with them as a pup. But his body had grown too tired.

On the day that Ted pulled himself onto a huge pile of the family's dirty washing, engulfed in the smells of them, his family, who loved him beyond words; they knew they had to make the decision for him. It was the hardest and most heartbreaking decision in the world, but the kindest thing they could do for him. It was time to let him rest.

The day was quiet - heavy. Everyone stayed close. Lexie stayed close to Ted, without words, her way of telling him he was the best boy, the bravest brother, the gentlest soul. Bill didn't bounce or bark. He knew. He stayed near, ears back, eyes wide, resting his head on Ted's paw.

The drive to the vet's was quiet. Too quiet. No excited panting, no nose smudges against the windows. Ted lay on Lexie's lap, wrapped in his favourite blanket, the one that smelled of home, smelled of Lexie, smelled of Bill, years of cuddles. His breathing was slow, his eyes gentle but tired. So very tired.

Bill sat beside him, unusually still. No whining, no wriggling. Just one soft paw resting against Ted's side, as if he knew. Maybe he did.

Lexie stayed still next to him the whole way. Maybe thinking about the games they played, the secrets they had shared, how he had always known when she needed him most. That they would love him forever.

Mum and Dad didn't speak. There weren't words big enough for what they felt. Ted had been their first baby. Their light in the darkness. Their comfort through storms. Their calm in the chaos.

As they neared the vet's, Bill let out the smallest whimper. Lexie reached over and held both her boys tighter.
Mum in tears gently whispered, "We're all here, Ted," she said softly. "your whole pack."

The sky outside was a dull grey, clouds hanging heavy like their hearts. The world, somehow, felt it too.

When they pulled into the car park, nobody moved straight away. Time slowed. A final moment of togetherness. One last ride.

As they carried him inside, Mum whispered, "Thank you, Ted. For every day. For all your love. For everything you have done for ME. We will carry you with us, always." She told him, through tears, how much he meant to them. That he had helped Mum and Dad, in ways few would every understand. Been their rock, their comfort, their first dog-shaped child.

Ted crossed the rainbow bridge in peace, safe, held, and surrounded by the people who adored him. His last breath was calm, knowing only love.

Bill curled up in the car on the way home, quiet and still. Something had changed. A piece of his world had gone. But he would carry Ted with him in every walk they had shared, every lesson he had learned, every cuddle he now gave a little more gently.

GRIEVEING TOGETHER

The house felt different without Ted. Quieter, colder somehow. His bed sat untouched. His bowls stayed put. None of them were ready to move them.

It was Bill who showed them the depth of loss. He searched the house over and over, nose pressed to the floor, sniffing in doorways, looking to corners, waiting. And then came the howling - long, aching sounds that none of them had ever heard before. He sat by the door, cried through the night, and pressed himself into Lexie's side like he could hold her sadness too.

Lexie, who had always been his person, was hurting in a way Bill could not fix. But that didn't stop him from trying.

Bill stayed close. If she cried, he licked her tears. If she curled into the settee, he curled tighter. If she disappeared into her room, Bill was right beside her, curling up on her bed, refusing to leave. They grieved together, girl and dog, each missing the same best friend.

Bill, still wild at heart, quieted for a while. No mischief, no zoomies. Just quiet presence. Silent understanding.

The house was too quiet, not just in sound, but in feeling. It was like the walls had stopped breathing. Like everything had paused, waiting. Ted was gone.
His bed still sat in the lounge, untouched. Mum couldn't move it. She walked past it ten times a day, glancing,

hoping, forgetting, then remembering. Every time, it felt like the breath caught in her chest all over again.

Bill didn't understand, not fully. He knew Ted was not coming back but he still lay beside his empty bed, nose pressed into the blanket that still smelled of his big brother. Bill would not eat, would not play, he just howled. Low and long, like his heart was cracking open with each howl he made. The kind of howl that broke through walls and broke hearts over and over again.

Lexie tried to be brave. She hugged Bill tight whispering into his fluffy ears, "I miss him too," but her eyes gave everything away.

Mum smiled for Lexie, held her sadness. Told her they would be okay. But when the house went quiet, and Lexie fell asleep the tears came into her pillow until she shook and finally fell asleep exhausted. Grief filled every corner.

They walked Ted's favourite walks, it felt wrong at first, too empty, too quiet. Like the wind should have carried his bark, like the trees should have waited for him. But they went anyway because not going, not taking Bill out for his walks hurt more.

One of Bill and Ted's nightly rituals was to share a carrot together, laid side by side in blissful silence. Bill would not eat his carrot without Ted with him. Lexie who never really liked food, for Lexie meals felt like effort. Textures too much, smells too strong. It wasn't her favourite part of the day. Then, one evening ,she asked mum for a carrot to share with Bill. There they sat, side by side, as Bill had done with Ted, sharing their carrot in blissful silence, no words needed. One carrot for her, one carrot for him. For those few quiet minutes, the world started to make sense once more.

And when Lexie finally smiled again, just a little, Bill's tail wagged for the first time in days. A tiny wag, but it was a start.

Ted had been Lexie's teacher, Bill's teacher, their brother, their protector.

Now it was Bill's turn.

The Biscuit Bin Men

Mum woke with a heavy heart to get through another day without their dear Ted. Every Friday, like clockwork, you could count on two things in their house, barking before 7am and the unmistakable rumble of the bin lorry making its way up the road.

Bill and Ted were never scared of the bin men, like most dogs. They loved the bin men. And the bin men? Well, they loved them right back.

Every Friday morning, Bill and Ted would walk Lexie to school. Mum in tow. They would hear them before they saw them. Bill would go into his usual overexcited whole-body wag. Ted would sit, calm, poised, both their tails thudding.

The truck would stop. The boys favourite "Biscuit Bin Man" would step out with his bag of treats and Bill and Ted would both get exactly what they wanted, treats and fuss.

That Friday was different. It was school holidays so no walk to school. And Ted, Ted was gone.

Bill still heard the bin truck, his tail wagged, he saw them through the window and barked.

Mum, still in her pyjamas, quietly said "No Bill, not today"!

The truck drew closer to home.

Bill barked again.

Again, Mum said, "NO Bill!"

Then Lexie, "Mum he wants to see the binmen, he wants his treat."

With a heavy heart and a weary smile, Mum said "Ok Lex, get his lead and take him outside."

Lexie, put Bill's lead on, looked at Mum and simply said, "Come with us." Lexie, who never asked for help, never wanted to show she too may need someone.

Mum looked at Lexie, with Bill sat at her feet, wagging his tail desperate to see his "biscuit bin men."

Mum, not wanting to, but knowing this is what Bill wanted, and Lexie needed, put on her coat, and stepped outside into the world.

The bin men saw Bill and Lexie.

The truck stopped.

The favourite "biscuit bin man" stepped out.

He looked around, then gently asked, "Where's the other fellow?"

37

Mum's voice caught in her throat. Tears in her eyes, "He's gone," she managed.

And without hesitation, this big, burly man in orange reached forward, and hugged her, really hugged her.

Then the whole crew came round. One by one. Quietly. Kindly.

"He was a great fellow," someone said. "I'm so sorry."

And right there, among bins, biscuits, and a waggy tail. Mum realised, Ted had not just touched their lives: Mum's, Dad's, and Lexie's. Ted had touched many lives and hearts. Even those of "the biscuit bin men" without them even knowing it.

The Sign from Ted

The house was still too quiet. Even with Bill's gentle cuddles and loving eyes, the space Ted once filled could not be ignored. Lexie, always wise (at times beyond her years), looked up at Mum one afternoon and said simply,

"Bill needs a brother, we are getting Bill a brother and we are calling him Bailey."

Mum smiled. Not just for her words, but the way Bill's ears perked up like he understood.

A few days later, Mum was scrolling through Facebook one evening and there it was, a post on Mums favourite "Cavachon UK" page asking for someone to rehome two Cavachons. "A bonded pair - Bailey and… Teddy."

Mum blinked at the names. A wave of warmth and sadness washed over her. Her arms filled with goosebumps. It was the names "Bailey and Teddy" she had not expected but knew in that moment, this was Ted's sign. Not a replacement. A continuation. A legacy.

After lots of phone calls between Mum and the amazing ladies from the "Cavachon UK Rehoming" page.

Videos sent of the house and garden that Bailey and Teddy could, possibly soon be calling their home.

Videos of Bill, on his best behaviour! Videos of Autumn on his best behaviour!

Mum received the phone call she had been waiting for. "Would you like to bring Bill and Lexie to come and meet Bailey and Teddy!" Of course, there was no question to ask.

Bill missed Ted terribly. He paced. He whined. He waited by the door like he was hoping Ted might just stroll back in and curl up like always.

Lexie had been lost too. It was time.

Now she just had to tell Dad.

Mum had been quiet, acting oddly for days. Cleaning and tidying the house, which Mum rarely did. That was Dad's domain.

Dad would return home from a long day at work to his favourite meals all ready and waiting for him, again Dad's domain. Mum even attempted to get the lawn mower out at one point to cut the grass but thought better of it. That was a step too far, again, Dad's domain.

Dad knew something was up and Mum was plotting something.

Not knowing that Mum had already been in secret talks with the "Cavachon UK Rehoming" page. Unaware that she had seen little brothers, Cavachon's like Bill, with the same curious eyes and wild hearts. Bailey and Teddy. A bonded pair. A double dose of trouble and love. Unaware that Mum already knew they were perfect.

Mum sat Dad down one evening with a cup of tea. That was always the warning sign.

"Just listen before you say no," she began.

Dad raised an eyebrow. "Right, what have you done now?"

Mum pulled out her phone and showed him their photo. Two mop-headed little misfits staring hopefully out of the screen.

Bailey, with his sideways grin.

Teddy, with his worried little eyes.

"They need us. They're in a foster home, and the rescue thinks we are perfect for them," Mum said.

Dad blinked. "Two? You want to bring home two more dogs?"

"They're a package deal," Mum replied firmly. "They've never been apart."

Dad stared at the screen again. Sighed. Looked at Bill curled up by Lexie's feet, a shadow of himself. Then sighed again, heavier this time. "Well," he muttered, "at least the house won't be quiet anymore."

Mum grinned. "That's not a yes, but I'm taking it as one."

By the next morning, the meeting was confirmed. Dad muttered something about needing stronger tea.

Mum ordered two new dog beds, a box of treats, and a mop.

Bill was bathed and groomed, Lexie even showered, which was not her favourite thing.

Mum, Lexie, and Bill made the seven hour round trip to meet the boys they had seen on the "Cavachon UK Rehoming" post. The boys that Ted had shown them to help them all move forwards.

Mum was nervous.

Lexie was fit to burst.

Bill was excited, although he didn't know why.

Something in the atmosphere had shifted, changed, everything suddenly felt lighter.

Mum was cautious trying to keep Lexie from exploding. "We must be gentle, Lex. Bailey and Teddy may be incredibly nervous. They may not like Bill, they may not like us." Lexie just scoffed and said "ok Mum" with the eyeroll just like her Dad.

They arrived at a park. Mum opened the door to the car and Bill shot out tail wagging like a helicopter. Lexie being pulled behind on his lead.

Bailey froze, then inched forwards, nose to nose with Bill. Barked once. Sniffed Bill, one sniff, two sniffs then a full body wag, a playful bounce and that was that. Instant partners in mischief.

Teddy hung back. Bill turned to him, gently. No bouncing. No barking. Just a slow tail and a little head tilt. He knew this look. Grief, uncertainty. He had worn it himself not long ago. Bill stepped closer, soft, calm and gave Teddy a little nuzzle. Teddy didn't run. He didn't hide. He simply leaned into it, the tiniest wag twitching at the tip of his tail.

Mum and Lexie brought them home.

Bailey, age six, all bright eyes and bounce.

And Teddy, age five, a quieter soul, with a knowing gaze.

Bailey and Teddy weren't sure what to make of their new home or Bill, at first. He was bouncy, barky, and overly friendly and they didn't know any of the house rules. Not that Bill followed many himself but, still, there were standards.

Within minutes of arriving, Bailey had stolen a sock from the laundry basket.

Bill had shown them both the treat cupboard.

Teddy, dear nervous Teddy, wasn't sure what to make of any of it. He just wanted to be loved.

Before long Bill was doing celebratory zoomies around the garden. Bailey joined him. Teddy tried, but he was so shy and confused he ran without knowing why.

Lexie laughed until she cried. It felt like the sun had come out again.

Sharing the settee was a whole new challenge.

Bailey liked to stretch out, like a prince. Teddy, unsure, nervous not knowing what to do, spun in circles before flopping on top of Bailey, and Bill… Bill was left teetering off the edge with his bum on one cushion and his head on Lexie's lap. But every night they found a way to squish together, three dogs, one child, one settee, and all the love in the world.

Autumn had retreated to the stairs to watch everything unfold from a safe distance, with a look of horror on his face as if to say, "What the hell have you done?"

Mum and Dad just looked and wondered where they were now meant to sit.

Before long, Bill was bounding through the house again, ears flying, toy in mouth, two new brothers tumbling after him.

Lexie laughed again.

Bill barked again.

And, the chaos, the joyful, muddy, barking, sock-stealing chaos was back.

Mum, Dad and Lexie continue to speak of Ted every day. His memories flow through the house.

The Lego flowers, that Dad and Lexie had put together for him, sit proudly in the fireplace along with the bandana he had got on a charity walk. His pawprint sits beside it.

The professional pictures, of Bill and Ted and another of Bill, Ted and Lexie, that Mum had won through a "dog pawtrait" competition adorn the walls in the lounge and kitchen.

But now, in honour of the love he gave, they share that love with Bailey and Teddy.

Ted would have approved.

The Other Side of the Chaos - Meet the Cats

While the Trio wreaked joyful havoc downstairs, there was once a quieter council in the house - A feline one. The original rulers of the home came with sharp claws, big personalities, and absolutely no tolerance for nonsense.

Summer. Autumn. Winter. The family's seasonal queen, king, and princess. Each with a role. Each with their own story.

Summer, the senior. 15, maybe 16 years old. Regal, wise, and over it.

When Bill burst into the house as a bearded baby hurricane, Summer sighed, flicked her tail, and made her way upstairs. She had seen it all before. She claimed the top floor as her retirement village, warm, peaceful, and 100% dog-free. A quiet life. A sunbeam nap. Her own food and water bowl.

Then... Bailey and Teddy arrived. Within a week, Summer had had enough. She was spotted trotting down the road like a woman on a mission. Not running away, just... relocating. She had chosen a new residence: an old lady's home a few doors down. One neighbour was spotted feeding her tuna. Another left her a soft cushion on a bench. Summer had retired from the chaos, officially. She had gone full pensioner cat. And her family, sad but didn't blame her.

Autumn however, stayed. Bill's original sidekick, his cat-burglar companion. Together, they had launched food raids, stared down squirrels, and tag-teamed the back of the settee.

When Bailey and Teddy showed up, Autumn glared. Hard. He did not leave like Summer; oh no, he stuck around to train the newbies.

Bailey got bopped.

Teddy got hissed at for sneezing too close.

It took a full year and a half, several rotisserie chickens, and enormous patience before Autumn allowed the two new boys into his realm.

Now, he tolerates them. Sometimes even shares the settee… briefly. But only on his terms.

Winter, the tiniest and quietest of the bunch, had come home in Mum's lunch bag from work one day. Again, Dad had not been told. He had come home from a busy day at work and there she was, this teeny tiny black kitten, full of fleas and worms. Dad said nothing, just sighed, rubbed his head and rolled his eyes again. He sat on the floor with her and tried to gain her trust.

Winter, the rescue, the size of a sandwich. She didn't make a sound. She didn't ask. She was simply happy to have a home. She lived in the shadows, a ghost with big eyes. Only when the house fell quiet at night would

Winter emerge. She would nudge Mum's hand in the dark, curl into her side, and purr with the softness of a soul who had finally found safety. She trusted no one else. Well, maybe Dad, if he didn't move.

As for the boys?

Bill was always over-familiar with Autumn, utterly oblivious to his boundaries. Autumn was Bills teammate.

Bailey tried to play and was immediately smacked.

Teddy cried every time a cat's paw hit the bottom of the stairs.

The boys learned to live around Autumn.

Autumn let them stay, but never let them forget who was boss.

And Winter? She watched from the stairs. She liked peace. Quiet. Mum? So yes, the house was full.

Dogs downstairs, creating havoc, cats upstairs, on patrol. Although Autumn would often visit downstairs.

Food still vanished; tuna mysteriously delivered down the road...

It was chaos. It was cuddles. It was them. One mad happy family.

And even though Summer chose peace, they think of her
every day; the wise one who knew when to exit the circus
and claim a life of quiet.

Smart girl, really.

Sharing Traditions

Bill had decided it was his job, his mission, to share all the traditions he and Ted had shared with his new brothers.

It began with socks. No one knew exactly when it began but at some point, a mysterious disappearance of socks became a household epidemic.

Bill, of course, was the mastermind. He didn't always do the stealing, but he supervised it.

Teddy, still unsure about the criminal underworld, mostly watched in awe. Though, on one occasion, he was spotted proudly parading a sock around the garden, so clearly the influence was spreading.

One by one, single socks vanished. Striped, fluffy, ankle-high, festive, no style was safe.

Lexie blamed the washing machine.

Mum blamed the laundry basket. But deep beneath the surface of domestic life… a sock-smuggling syndicate had formed.

It was Bailey.

Operating under cover of cuteness, Bailey would patrol the downstairs rooms with a trained eye. If a sock was left anywhere, on the sofa, beside the laundry basket, under the radiator, he struck. Quietly. Swiftly. Without remorse.

The stash? Hidden deep in the boys' bed what the family began referring to as Sock Heist Headquarters. There, buried among chewed toys and half-eaten biscuits, were trophies: socks of every size and scent.

When the hoard was discovered one afternoon, after Mum ran out of socks again, Bailey simply wagged. Unapologetic. Triumphant. Somewhere in the corner, Bill gave a slow blink of approval.

Mission accomplished.

From that day forward, every missing sock had only one explanation: BAILEY!

Bills Next Mission – Introduce his new brothers to the "Biscuit Bin Men".

He sat proudly at the end of the driveway, with Lexie, tail wagging like a flag. "Wait," he seemed to say, "Just wait, they're coming."

Bailey was instantly on board, barking, bouncing, Mum did not stop him.

Teddy, on the other hand, heard the noise and immediately panicked. He launched into full "They've come to take me away!" mode, howling, spinning, hiding behind Mum's legs like the bin men were the end of days.

The truck screeched to a halt.

Out stepped the "Biscuit Bin Man," same bag of treats, same warm grin. "Bill!" he called cheerfully, handing over the usual treat.

Bailey launched forward and snatched the entire bag.

Teddy let out a scream that could curdle milk and bolted into Mum's legs.

The "biscuit bin man" just stared… and then burst out laughing.

"Oh my god," he said, tears of laughter in his eyes. "You've got your hands full now!"

Mum smiled, slightly grimaced, still trying to reassure Teddy that the world was not about to end. Watching Bill proudly share his ritual.

Bill's Next Mission - the evening carrot.

Once a sacred ritual between Bill and Ted, now had three eager faces waiting patiently in the kitchen. Bill still took his first, of course. He had earned that right. But then, with a little nudge of his nose and a glance at Mum, the next carrot went to Bailey and then Teddy. A tradition once shared by two was now reborn in a trio, honouring the memory of the brother who came before.

Given every night, the same way, in the same order.

Bill - Bailey - Teddy.

Bill became the unspoken guide. Not always graceful, not always subtle, but always present.

He taught Teddy how to settle on the settee. After much trial and error, mostly involving Teddy hovering nervously on the floor, while Bill sighed dramatically from the cushions. Bailey was quicker, he did not wait to be invited. He leapt straight onto the softest spot like he owned the place. Bill tolerated it… barely.

On walks, Bill showed them the "Important Smells," The Good Tree, The Stranger's Garden, and of course, The Favourite Bin. Bailey caught on quickly and marked them as his own. Teddy took longer, still shy, still cautious, but Bill waited, always circling back for him.

Bill's Next Mission – The big stuff.

He showed them how to spot a picnic from a mile off, how to pretend not to hear Mum shouting, "NOOOO!" as they made a beeline for the naan breads and sausage rolls. He shared the joy of a perfectly timed protest pee, especially if Mum was watching.

And when Teddy barked the entire way to a new place, Bill didn't scold. He just gave him a look, the same one Ted once gave him, as if to say, "It is scary now, but you will love it soon."
And, he did.

Bill taught them the art of being there for Lexie. How to sit close but not too close. How to listen without speaking. How to nudge her hand gently in those quiet, uncertain moments when words felt too big.

Bailey brought the comedy.

Teddy needed the comfort.

Bill brought the experience.

All the wonderful, joyous, chaotic experiences his big brother Ted had taught him.

Bill was now paying them forward.

The traditions passed on quietly. Through looks. Through sniffs. Through mayhem. Through love.

And somewhere between the howls, the sock heists, the bin raids, and the belly-up naps, the three of them became a team.

A trio. A family.

It was not the same. It never would be.

Ted no longer with them. Not physically, anyway.

But the love, the connection, the magic of those little moments?

Still there. Everyday. Biscuit included.

They moved forwards.

The Pre-Walk Panic

Every dog loves a walk.

Teddy, however, takes his walks to the extreme, Teddy thinks walks are the meaning of life.

It didn't take Mum or Lexie long to discover just how much Teddy LOVED his walks. It was as though walks were Teddy's destiny.

It starts with the first clue, the boys have all had breakfast, Mum has stood up, Teddy knows, no words need to be uttered, God forbid at this point the "W" word is mentioned. Mum doesn't even have to put on a shoe or touch a lead, or casually check she has enough poo bags.

Teddy explodes. Not just barking. Ear-piercing, high-octane, frantic wailing that echoes off the walls like an air raid siren made of fluff. His paws do a little tap dance, his eyes go wide, and he spins in tight circles like he is powered by espresso.

Bill and Bailey? Calm. Experienced. Waiting by the door like civilised lads.

Teddy? Teddy is having a full-on emotional breakdown.

"MUM'S GOT THE COAT!! THE COAT MEANS OUTSIDE!! THE WORLD EXISTS!! I MUST BARK UNTIL MY FACE FALLS OFF!!"

Mum tries to shush him.

Lexie shouts, "TEDDY, IT'S HAPPENING, CALM DOWN!!"

Dad puts his finger in his only functioning ear yelling "I've only got one ear that works, Jeysus Christ Teddy!"

But Teddy can't. He won't. He is in too deep. By the time the lead clips on, Teddy's entire body is vibrating with joy. Mum's head is ringing saying "Oh My God, this is not normal behaviour, what is wrong with him?"

By the time the door opens, everything is a blur. Teddy outside is bursting with excitement, he is out in the world again like it was the first walk he has ever had.

By the time they reach the end of the drive, he is finally quiet... panting, proud, and deeply satisfied that his performance was once again Tony Award-winning.

Neighbours have asked, "Is he okay?"

That's just Teddy, getting ready for his walk. Every. Single. Day.

Three Leads, No Control

Mum soon discovered whilst walking three dogs sounded like a lovely idea, fresh air, wagging tails, happy family outings. In reality? Uproar. Pure, exhausting, sometimes hilarious uproar.

Lead walking -

Walking one dog - Manageable.

Walking two dogs - Tricky.

Walking three dogs - An Olympic event requiring grit, flexibility, and the reflexes of a ninja.

Every morning, Mum took a deep breath, triple checked each lead, clipped the boys in … and muttered a quiet, desperate "Please behave." To the universe. It never listened.

Bill marched ahead like he had a purpose, charging full steam ahead like a small, furry steam train. Convinced he was going to miss his station if he wasn't fast enough.

Bailey zigzagged like a pinball machine, chasing leaves, smells, and shadows.

Teddy? Teddy spotted a leaf. A harmless, fluttering leaf. And froze. Then whimpered. Then sat down like he had just witnessed something traumatic in a David Attenborough documentary.

The leads tangled instantly. Mum spun like she was in a three-dog maypole dance, her arms flailing. Her legs got knotted tighter with every step, and as she tried to untwist herself,

Bailey decided to do a full-body shake, sending Teddy into turmoil.

Bill, meanwhile, leapt up to bark at a squirrel (which may have been a stick).

And Teddy pulled backwards to escape a terrifying passing jogger.

And Mum she was already used to the daily public embarrassment, she'd hit the deck more than once. Leads in her hand muttering, "It's fine, it's fine, I'm fine." into the pavement while the boys licked her like she was a fallen ice cream.

Mum would hit the ground with a spectacular splat, once flat on her face, once flat on her back.

A dog walker would stare, but continued walking.

Mum would witness curtains twitching as the locals watched the daily entertainment from the comfort of their homes.

And as the boys would finish the licking ceremony, realise Mum was in fact fine.

Bill would cock his head with a look that said, "Well, you should have just let go of the leads then."

Bailey, utterly unapologetic, would lick her nose and try to climb on her chest.

And Teddy would peek out from under her legs, trembling but curious, as if to ask, "Is this what a walk is supposed to be?"

By the end of the walk, the boys would be panting and happy.

Mum would have brushed herself off, got back on her feet, and resumed some sense of control.

Because this was life walking three dogs. Messy, tangled, loud, and absolutely perfect.

The Car of Doom

Once Teddy was out of the house and on his walk, calm usually resumed. Usually.

But then came… the car. At first, Mum had thought they had struck gold. That first journey home from meeting Teddy and Bailey was quiet. Blissfully, suspiciously quiet. No barking, no howling, no commotion. Teddy had curled up beside Bill like a little lost lamb.

"See?" Mum smiled to herself. "He's a dream." Oh Mum, bless her optimism. That silence was not peace. It was confusion. Fear. Shell-shocked, don't-make-a-sound kind of nerves.

Within a week the car had become the frontline of war. Now settled and a little more confident, Teddy was starting to find his paws. He had also discovered something incredible. The real Teddy… had found his voice. It became a pattern.

Every car journey started calm. Settled. Tranquil. Until five minutes before arriving.

It didn't matter where: the park, the woods, the shops, even Norfolk or Cornwall. Five minutes from the destination and the symphony of doom began.

It started with little whines, then escalated, then exploded.

First: Teddy.

High-pitched. Long. Desperate. A sound that could shatter glass and trigger car alarms.

"ARRROOOOO-WOOOOO-WOOO!"

Next: Bailey. Chiming in like a backup singer on fast-forward, trying to out-bark his brother just for fun.

Finally: Bill. With a slow-building, mournful husky-howl that could summon wolves from the wild.

It was… catastrophic. An ear splitting, operatic, chilling shrill.

Dad would slam his finger into his good ear and attempt to drive with one hand.

Lexie would shriek, "Abort! Abort!" Throwing herself over Bill's ears to shield him from the frenzy. Though it was usually Bill contributing to it.

Mum? Mum stared out the window, whispering prayers to the gods of sanity and earplugs.

And then, the moment of arrival. The car would screech into a parking space.

Doors would burst open. Mum, Dad, and Lexie would tumble out like survivors of a natural disaster.

Inside the car? Three unhinged, screaming dogs.

Onlookers watched with wide eyes and dropped jaws.

One woman in the park car park once muttered, "Is that a… mobile kennel?!"

Another whispered, "Are they okay?"

To which Mum simply laughed and replied, "Yes, yes they are just excited."

Mum assessed every theory, maybe it was the indicator, NOPE, Speed bump, NOPE, Google maps voice, NOPE. Teddy had a built in sixth sense that knew exactly when the car was going to stop, and the FUN was going to begin.

And yet, no matter how chaotic, how ear-splitting, how utterly absurd it got… They would not change a thing.

Because those howls? That anarchy? That unfiltered, passionate, ridiculously timed noise?

It meant Teddy had found his voice. Found his place. Found his family.

Even if it meant blowing out every eardrum along the way.

Teddy the Scared Little Soul

When Teddy first arrived, he didn't seem to know what safety felt like. He didn't trust it. Didn't believe in it. Didn't believe in himself.

His world had changed overnight, new home, new people, strange smells, and a brother named Bailey who, from the start, looked like he belonged.

But Teddy? He wasn't sure. Those first evenings were quiet. He sat near the settee, puffing, panting, pacing. too frightened to lie down, too unsure to be still. Lexie sat beside him, whispering soft things.

Mum gave him space.

Bill watched from his favourite corner with a slow blink, like he knew this was going to take time. He didn't bark. He didn't beg. He didn't make a fuss. He just waited.

But Teddy Worried. Guarded. As if the love might be taken away at any moment.

The first trip to the vet was heartbreaking.

Bailey bounced in like he owned the place.

Teddy shook.

Not just a little. His whole body trembled, tail tucked, ears flat, eyes wide with silent panic.

He pressed himself into Mum's legs. Then into the corner. Then under the bench.

The vet knelt down gently. Teddy peed everywhere. The vet could not examine him. Teddy was too afraid. Too frozen. Too unsure if this was going to be the moment everything fell apart again. They didn't force it. They took him home, wrapped him in a blanket, and let him hide... until he did not need to anymore.

Teddy hates the vet. He probably always will. He tucks his tail. Shakes like he's made of leaves. Looks at Mum with wide eyes like, "Please, not this again."

And every single time, Mum whispers, "It's okay, Teddy, I'm right here."

But the difference is, he no longer faces it alone. Because being brave isn't about not being scared, it's about having someone who loves you enough to sit through the fear with you.

Teddy finally has that. He slowly, so slowly began to believe. That food would come. That soft voices meant kindness. That hands could be gentle. That love was real. That this home, this settee, these people... were his.

Now? Teddy curls beside Mum, like he has always been there. He goes to the vet with his tail cautiously wagging. He still checks. Still hesitates. But he trusts just enough to try.

And, every day, he lets a little more love in. Because scared little souls? They do not stay scared forever. Not when they are finally home.

The Grooming Incident

Mum had always handled grooming like a pro. She had always groomed Ted and Bill herself. A snip here, a brush there, job done.

Ted would sit like a gentleman. Ted was calm.

Bill was Bill, but manageable, he would fidget a bit, roll over dramatically, and pretend to die at the sight of a nail file, but overall? Manageable, nothing Mum couldn't handle with a towel, a treat, and sheer willpower.

So naturally, when Bailey and Teddy joined the family, she thought, "How hard can it be?"

Answer: Very! She set the scene: Clippers, scissors, brush, towel, treats. Dog-friendly playlist on. Calm voice: "This will be fine."

She started with Bailey. Brush in hand. Clippers ready. Bailey took one look at the setup, gave her a single raised eyebrow, and walked out of the room like a man who absolutely would not be participating in this nonsense. When she followed him with the clippers? He side-eyed her like she had deeply offended his ancestors.

Then came Teddy. Sweet, gentle, anxious Teddy. Mum didn't even turn the clippers on. She showed them to him. Held them up with a calm voice: "It's okay, Teddy. Just a little trim." Teddy screamed. A high-pitched, operatic,

"SOMEONE IS TRYING TO MURDER ME WITH ELECTRIC BLADES!" type scream.

He ran. He leapt. He jumped off the grooming table.

Bailey joined in, whether in sympathy or confusion, no one knows.

Bill barked once and went back to his spot with a sigh like, "Amateurs."

The clippers were gently placed back in the drawer.

The next week, they went to a professional groomer. Mum dropped them off with their little bags of treats. She handed over the dogs with a sheepish smile and a nervous laugh. "They're… sensitive," she said, explaining her boys' story.

Bailey padded in, already judging everything.

Teddy had to be gently convinced. Twice.

Mum left, anxious and worried but with the blissful idea that she might enjoy a cup of tea in peace.

An hour passed. No call.

Two hours. Still nothing.

Three. She texted: "All okay?"

The reply: "Almost there…"

When she finally returned, the groomer stepped out of the back room like someone who had aged fifteen years.

"They're… done," she said, hair in her eyes, slightly trembling. "At last."

Bailey emerged first, looking half regal, half furious.

Teddy came out second, looking traumatised and somehow smaller, like he'd emotionally deflated.

Mum stared at them both. "You were in there four hours? What on earth happened?"

The groomer just said, "They have strong opinions."

Bailey strutted out like he had filed a HR complaint.

Teddy climbed into the car and refused to make eye contact.

Mum handed over extra tip money, a nervous thank-you, and mentally vowed, "Next time I'll send Bill for moral support."

When they got home, Bailey immediately rolled in the grass.

Teddy tried to crawl into his bed backwards.

Bill sniffed them, blinked slowly, and returned to his spot as if to say, "Now do you see why I roll in fox poo?" Now? The three boys go together, arriving like a scruffy, slightly nervous boy band on tour.

Bill struts in first, tail wagging like a metronome.

Bailey follows, bouncing to his own beat.

And Teddy? He still hesitates, still looks up at Mum for reassurance but he goes in because his brothers are there, and he knows they will come out together.

What once took four hours now takes half the time. No drama, no tangled tails. Just three very handsome, fluffy, sweet-smelling boys bursting out of the salon like they have been to a spa treatment.

And Mum whispers lovingly, "Look at you all." Trying to sniff and kiss each of them. Bailey usually licks his paw and wipes it on Bill. Teddy jumps into Mum's lap. Bill Jumps on Bailey. Before Mum wrestles them into the car and the clean chaos continues.

Meeting the Mates

The moment Mum turned onto the gravel lane that led to what had at one time been the big open training field, Bill knew. His tail started thumping against the car door like a drumroll. His eyes sparkled with anticipation. And by the time the car had pulled to a halt, he practically launched himself into the air, paws skidding in excitement as he landed on the grass.

Today was special. Today, he was introducing Bailey and Teddy to his dog mates. Not just any mates either - Bobby and Bunty

Bobby, a fellow Cavachon and loyal partner in play, always up for a good wrestle or a mad zoomie could give Bailey a run for his money.

And then there was Bunty, the Bedlington Terrier with legs for days, a constant twinkle in her eye, and the type of flirty swagger that could melt the fur off a Labrador. She adored Bill. The feeling was mutual.

Bill sprinted ahead, barking in excitement as he spotted them already on the field, tails wagging, waiting like a welcoming committee.

Bailey, naturally, exploded from the car like a firework, barking just to hear the sound of his own voice. Teddy hesitated, hopping nervously out and immediately gluing himself to Mums leg.

Lexie, ever patient with the boys, gave him a soft smile and whispered, "It's okay, they're Bill's people."

Bill was already halfway through his welcoming parade, bouncing up to Bobby with a playful bark before circling Bunty with the kind of energy that made it noticeably clear he was showing off.

He darted back toward his brothers with a dramatic spin, like a tour guide ready to present the newest members of his pack. He stood proudly between them, puffed out like he had just won an award.

"This is Bailey," he seemed to say with a bounce of his head, "Complete menace - partial to socks."

"And this is Teddy - nervous, sweet, and full of surprises. Trust me, he is coming out of his shell."

Bobby gave Bailey a sniff and an approving tail wag before lunging into a game of chase, which Bailey happily joined, crashing into a cone within seconds and then pretending it hadn't happened.

Bunty slinked up to Bill, brushing her side dramatically against his and fluttering her tail like a feathery fan.

Teddy stared, bewildered. Lexie gave him a gentle nudge forward. He took a cautious step. Then another. Bunty gave him a soft bop on the nose, then turned her flirty antics back on Bill, who was now trying to race Bobby and Bailey around the field and losing badly.

Teddy wandered toward the water bowl, looked back at Lexie, and sat calmly in the shade. It was enough. Small steps. Big wins.

Mum stood at the edge of the field; arms crossed but smiling. "He's so proud," she said to Bobby and Bunty's mums. "He's showing off like he built this place," they chuckled.

And honestly? He kind of had. This field was where Bill had learned, grown, made his first doggy friendships. Now he was the one doing the introductions. The bridge between old mates and new beginnings.

Eventually, the zoomies slowed. Bobby lay flopped in a patch of clover. Bunty stretched.

It was the moment Bill had been waiting for - introducing his new brothers to his best mates, Bobby and Bunty.

The place where the mums had got in trouble. Where the six of them had started a mutiny in solidarity. The place where they were once told there was too much chatting. Too much laughing. Too much, "Oh well, they're happy!" and not nearly enough actual training.

The place where the instructor had agreed that, "Yes you may all be happier somewhere else." The place where now Bailey and Teddy were joining Bill, Bobby, and Bunty for what was now unofficial "training club." No pressure. No sit-stays. Just long walks, good gossip, and the occasional pub lunch.

The place where the dogs thrived. The mums relaxed. And a lifelong friendship had been formed, both human and furry.

Teddy and the Pub Lunch Initiation

There comes a time in every dog's life when they must face the rite of passage. For some, it is chasing their first squirrel. For others, it is stealing their first slipper.

But in Bill, Bailey, and Teddy's family it was surviving your first pub trip. It was now a tradition for Bill, Bobby and Bunty - a badge of honour. So now it was Bailey and Teddy's turn.

Bill was excited, too excited. As soon as he heard the three sacred words, "Bobby, Bunty, Pub" he did three full laps around the kitchen, then sat by the front door vibrating like a phone on silent.

But Teddy? This was unfamiliar territory.

First Mum and Lexie had to go through the ear piecing rigmarole of just getting Teddy out the house and into the car. Teddy realising he was going out in the world again for Mum and Lexie, that was an "experience" in itself. Teddy now knew what the "W" word meant which sent him into his own magical hysterics, Teddy had learned to love a car ride.

But "PUB" was a new code word, and it made Teddy deeply unsure. Such a simple word "pub" NOONE was prepared for the pub.

They parked the car. Teddy looked nervous. They clipped on leads. Teddy froze. They opened the pub door... Teddy lost his mind.

Bailey had never been in a pub before. Teddy had barely made peace with garden furniture. So naturally, the moment they stepped foot into the pub...

All hell broke loose.

Teddy screamed. Not barked, screamed. Like a toddler who had dropped their ice cream, type scream. A long, high pitched, panicked wail that echoed through the building like a fire alarm of fluff. That silenced the entire establishment. Conversations stopped, cutlery paused mid-air, eyes turned. Lexie froze.

Teddy had made up his mind the "Pub" was terrifying and EVERYONE needed to know.

Customers turned. Staff blinked. A dog at another table dropped his chew. Someone spilled a pint. Mum attempted snacks. Nothing worked. Teddy was convinced he had entered the gates of hell. Clearly, Teddy was not ready for the world of pub lunches.

Bill judged.

Bailey sulked.

Bobby, and Bunty looked at the new boys like they had just ruined a sacred tradition.

Mum attempted calm. Lexie whispered, "It's okay, Teddy…" while frantically unwrapping a dog treat. But it was no use. The mission was quickly aborted.

Everyone retreated outside, faces red, ears ringing. But they did not give up.

The next time, they sat outside. Far away from the building.

Teddy still barked, still paced, still gave serious "we are all going to die" vibes, but slightly less than last time.

Then came the breakthrough.

Lexie, expert at quiet bribery, sneakily passed a chip under the table. Teddy sniffed it. Paused. Ate it. Paused again. And wagged. Two more chips. A nibble of her hot dog. Lexie did not like eating anyway, and Teddy was happy. Well, happier. Pub lunch stopped being terrifying. It became… delightful.

Now, Teddy trots in behind Bill, Bailey, Bobby, and Bunty like a pub pro. He curls under the table, keeps one eye on Lexie (a.k.a. The Chip Source), and accepts every morsel like a very polite prince. From that day on, Teddy was in.

Pub lunches? Part of the routine. Chips? His new currency. And the best part?

The mums never stopped chatting. The dogs never stopped begging.

And Lexie? She just smiled, knowing that, once again Teddy had found his place.

Once Teddy had realised that pubs were not scary, he would fully leaned in. He knew how it worked now: arrive, sniff things, watch Bill work the room like a seasoned local, get a few chips, lie under the table, occasionally nuzzle Lexie's knee for moral support.

It was… actually okay. But there was one rule Teddy had made very clear:

Once the chips are gone - so is Teddy.

At first it started small. A little shuffle. A tiny sigh. A paw on Mums leg. Then came the soft whine, like a distant kettle beginning to boil. And then the howl. It built like a dramatic crescendo in a musical. From one quiet yawn-like grumble to full-blown operatic wailing, complete with barking interludes. His own, very vocal, very public way of saying:

"I'M DONE NOW. I WOULD LIKE TO GO HOME."

Other dogs might snore. Others might nudge their owners with a paw. Not Teddy.

Teddy preferred to cause an incident. And this day was no different.

The pub was busy. Mum had just settled into another conversation with Bobby and Bunty's mums. Bill was dozing under the table, one ear flicking at every mention of "chip". Bailey was trying to subtly edge his way into someone else's plate. Bunty was curled up under a stranger's chair like she owned them.

Teddy had eaten his chip. His last chip. He had tried to lie down. But the chips had stopped. And so began the song. A single howl. Then another, louder. A bark. Another. Then louder again, until half the pub were whispering, heads turning, pints halfway to lips, eyebrows raised, confusion blooming across faces.

Mum stood up. Calm. Steady. The howling reached its peak. Someone muttered, "What's wrong with the dog?"

Without flinching, without apology, Mum lifted her chin and addressed the room. The entire Pub! "Teddy is a rescue," she said, voice clear and strong. "He's doing so well, but he's had enough now. He is telling me it is time to go home."

The effect was instant. The frowns melted. The whispers turned into quiet smiles. Heads nodded. Someone murmured, "Bless him." Another person clapped softly. A man by the fireplace leaned in and said, "What a brave boy."

Mum collected Teddy's lead, patted his head, and whispered, "I am so proud of you. Well done, Teddy."

And off they walked, past the bar, through the crowd, heads high. By the time Mum had tucked him into the back of the car, blanket fluffed, little chew toy beside him, tail wagging softly, Teddy was already settling down with a sigh of contentment. Mission accomplished.

Mum returned to the pub, cool as anything, scooped up the remaining dogs and Lexie, and waved goodbye to the now-adoring pub-goers.

Bobby and Bunty's mums had already paid the bill. Bunty had apparently adopted a couple from Yorkshire.

Mum smiled to herself. Maybe, just maybe, this had been Teddy's plan all along.

These days, Mum barely flinched at the routine. She knew the signs. Knew his limits. Knew when it was time to leave. She stood tall. Sure. Proud of him, proud of them all. Because progress was not always neat. Sometimes it was messy. Sometimes it howled.

But it was always worth it.

Partners in Grime

Just as things were starting to settle with Bailey and Teddy finding their paws, Bill decided it was time to shake things up again.

Bailey had started small, sneaking socks from the laundry basket and leaving them in Teddy's bed.

Then came the lunch incident. Lexie had just stepped away for a moment when Bill and Bailey launched a tag-team operation. Bailey distracted Lexie with puppy eyes, while Bill knocked the plate off the chair. By the time anyone noticed, Teddy was covered in crumbs and looking very confused.

Bill, now the seasoned mischief-maker, took it upon himself to teach Bailey all the "important" things, like how to tear open the post, or that squeaky toys are not truly dead until the stuffing is everywhere.

But even as the chaos returned, it was filled with laughter.

Teddy began to relax, tail wagging a little more each day. Although he still jumped at loud noises or hid when visitors came. He had Bill by his side, always nudging him forward. Showing him, how fun life could be when you had a family who loved you no matter what.

Bill had finally got his mojo back. With Bailey and Teddy by his side, he had not one but two partners in crime.

It started off quietly. A shredded toilet roll here, a slipper mysteriously relocated there. But the real turning point came one afternoon when Mum dared to leave them alone in the kitchen. The bins did not stand a chance.

When Mum opened the door, it looked like a food-fight tornado had passed through. Pasta, wrappers, tea bags, bits of veg, potatoes. Mum had just cleaned Bunny out before she left the house and placed the waste safely, or so she thought, in another bin. Included in the mess, sawdust, wet pee, and poo-soaked sawdust - All Over the Floor.

And in the middle of it sat Bill, looking proud as punch.

Bailey peeked out from under a blanket with crumbs on his nose.

Teddy? Found later in the dog bed surrounded by what used to be a loaf of bread.

It was chaos. It was carnage. And it was absolutely classic Bill, teaching his new brothers the fine art of mischief.

And as Lexie's mum took a deep breath, Bill gave her his best innocent eyes. It didn't work. But it almost did. They had only just begun. If you thought Bill, alone, was trouble, just wait until you meet the fully formed trio.

They were unstoppable. With Teddy growing braver and Bailey getting bolder by the day, Bill officially had his dream team assembled.

THE TURD HEAD TRIO was born, and they had one mission: turn peace and quiet into a distant memory. It started with the bin raid, but that was just the warm-up act.

The next day Mum made the rookie mistake of leaving the boys in the kitchen whilst she went out for a well-earned relaxing coffee. The boys had been walked, they were all happy and sleepy what could possibly go wrong? Surely lighting wouldn't strike twice?

As Mum parked outside the café, she made the swift decision to quickly look at the kitchen cameras to check her boys were all ok. Checking the cameras, she saw them in action, again. Bins tipped. Wrappers flying.

Teddy gleefully nosing through crumbs like he had just discovered treasure.

Bill was already doing zoomies through the destruction.

And Bailey? Bailey was making merry hell. Mum knew what he was going to do before it even happened. "The Protest Pee" Mum pressed the speaker to yell at him in horror.

"BAILEY, NO. BAILEY, STOP!"

Bailey looked directly at the camera. Made eye contact with Mum and without hesitation. Bailey cocked his leg and…. peed up the bin. No amount of Mum shouting through the speaker made a difference. The boys were in the zone. They were artists. And this? This was their masterpiece.

Later, when Mum came home and opened the door, all three dogs greeted her like nothing had happened, wagging tails, innocent faces, and just the faintest hint of bin juice in the air.

They were gross. They were proud. They were unstoppable.

Bill had taken his new role seriously, he was not just the lead troublemaker anymore, he was "the" teacher.

Teddy followed him everywhere, still cautious, but no longer trembling.

Bailey, cheeky and fearless, was learning fast, especially the art of stealth sock-snatching and carnage maker.

Lexie watched it all unfold with both exasperation, joy, and pride. Her heart was healing. And somehow, in all the madness, so was Bill's.

But the best part? Despite the destruction, every photo taken, had one thing in common: three grinning dogs, sitting shoulder-to-shoulder like furry bandits after a successful heist. Mum didn't know whether to laugh or cry.

Lexie laughed. A lot. Bill was back. And now he had backup.

Back to Ted's Beach

It was their first proper summer holiday together.

Lexie, Bill, Bailey, and Teddy.

Mum had only one destination in mind: Perranporth. Ted's beach. The place they had last holidayed with Ted.

Mum smiled as they turned off the familiar road. She could still see the photos in her mind: Dad red-faced, hauling the overloaded beach cart up Cardiac Hill like a determined packhorse, bodyboards, wetsuits, windbreakers, three chairs, two buckets, three spades, mismatched towels... and Ted, wrapped in a blanket, perched like a tiny, royal beach lord on his cushion when he got too tired to walk. Ted had loved that cart ride. From his high seat, he would watch Lexie and Bill charge down to the tide, barking and splashing, while he simply soaked it all in, like a king surveying his kingdom.

And now, it was time to share that kingdom with the new boys.

Teddy, however, did not approve of the packing stage. The moment the suitcases appeared, he shrieked like a banshee. "They're leaving me! They're leaving me!"
He threw himself dramatically at the front door, howling like he was being abandoned to a life of sorrow. Mum gave in early, opened the car door, and put him in first, blanket, toy, and all. Then just packed around him. Step by step, while he watched with big, suspicious eyes just

85

to make sure they did not forget anyone. Especially not him.

Bailey was a tornado of excitement. Buckets? Spades? He dragged them all into the kitchen, then out into the garden. Last year's sand exploded everywhere, on the rug. Into Mum's washing basket. He didn't care. He was going on an adventure.

Bill, seasoned pro, simply watched the mayhem and wagged his tail. He knew what this meant: sand. sea. chips, ice cream. Cornish pasty crumbs, and if he was lucky, a second breakfast from Dad's dropped sausage sandwich.

They arrived at the same caravan, parked in the same spot that overlooked the same windy footpath down to the bay. And it was like stepping into a memory. The same river trickling down to the sea that Ted had loved to lie in, cooling off in the shallows, while the others gallivanted about. The same chip shop, where Ted had once "accidentally" snatched a chip midair. The same ice cream stand, where he had licked Mum's cone so fast, she hadn't noticed until she was eating just wafer.

Now, Bailey stuck his head right into the river and came up with a leaf stuck to his nose.

Teddy tiptoed into the shallows and then squealed as if he had stepped on a sea monster.

Bill? Bill just ran. Full pelt. Down the beach. Ears flying, tail up, freedom in his bones.

Mum watched them all and whispered, "Ted would have loved this. They are carrying him with them."

Later, they all sat on "Ted's beach," with Ted's cart (still overstuffed), this time with Teddy curled up in the cart, thinking, "They have to take the cart, they have to take me!"

Bill digging a trench that would make Ted proud.

Bailey guarding the snack bag like his life depended on it.

It was not the same, but it was still beautiful, because Ted's beach was not just a memory now, it was a legacy being passed on, pawprint by pawprint, heart by heart.

Back at the caravan, things quickly descended into... well, the usual carnage. The boys thundered in like they owned the place.

Bill jumped straight on the sofa bed, wet and sandy, spinning in four tight circles before flopping down with a dramatic sigh.

Bailey found a half-eaten dog biscuit under a cupboard and spent ten minutes guarding it from nobody.

Teddy, naturally, screamed when Mum left the caravan to get the bedding, without him! He stared at the caravan door like it had betrayed him, howling until she reappeared holding his blanket.

Lexie laughed, flopped onto the bed with them, and declared it the best caravan in the world.

Mum agreed. Dad looked at the trail of sand and sighed, already mentally vacuuming it.

The next day, the Perranporth Chaos Tour resumed. They visited all the classics, starting with the onsite shop where Bill and Ted had sat quietly and patiently with Dad waiting for Mum and Lexie to reappear with, as Dad called it their bag of "God knows what!"

This time, Dad was waiting outside with Bill, Bailey, and Teddy!

Teddy soon realised Mum had entered "The Black Hole" without him! MUM HAD DISSAPPEARED! Cue the drama:

Teddy started wailing, a full Teddy special. Head back, eyes wide, front paws thumping the pavement as he let out a desperate tortured, "WAAAAAAAAAHHH!" Mum could hear him from inside the shop.

People stopped and stared.

Dad looked as though he had no idea who this dog belonged to, even though he was holding the lead.

Mum and Lexie finally reappeared, holding a bag of "God knows what".

Dad muttering "What took you so long?" Holding Teddy's lead out as if to say, "Just take him, he's YOUR dog."

Teddy gasped. Let out one final wail of betrayal. Then sat wondering why everyone was staring!

Bailey didn't even look up, he was busy trying to charm a sausage roll off a stranger.

Bill lay down with a groan like a long-suffering bodyguard.

A woman passing by asked Dad if he was ok! Dad was unsure if they were talking to him or asking about the dog.

Mum completely unfazed, replied "He's fine, he thought I had been abducted!"

Lexie sighed, gently patting Teddy's head.

They continued - The ice cream shop, where Teddy refused to try a doggy cone, but accepted a lick of Mum's after pretending he didn't want it.

Ted's river, where the three of them waded in together.
Bill lay in the middle like a soggy king, Bailey splashed around digging holes, and Teddy, again, tiptoed in,

slipped, shrieked, then got out and sulked next to Mum until he was wrapped in a towel.

That afternoon, they walked the coastal path, windy and wild. Bill took the lead, head high, as if showing Bailey and Teddy the route that Ted used to walk with him. Lexie running ahead as she always did. Dad muttered about the incline and tried to stop Bailey from eating sheep poo.
Teddy refused to walk at all unless Mum held his lead. Mum didn't argue.

On the final evening, Lexie collected a bottle of sand from "Ted's beach" to take home for him. Lexie held the little bottle of sand close. Bailey curled up beside her. Teddy rested his chin on Mum's lap. Bill sat perfectly still, eyes on the sunset.

Mum said, softly, "Same beach. Same sky. We came back. They love it here too. We miss you, Ted."

The Rise of the Turd Head Trio

With Bailey firmly established as the resident sock thief.

Teddy learning to trust more each day.

And Bill, back to his old bouncy self, something magical happened.

Mum decided it was time to share the joy, and chaos that these boys brought, with the world. Or, at least, with the "Cavachon UK" dog community.

Through Mum's favourite Facebook page "Cavachon UK," began the Cavachon Walks, which quickly took on their more accurate (and affectionately ridiculous) title:

"Turd Head Walks."

It was meant to be a simple group stroll for Cavachon owners, but when people heard that Bill, Bailey, and Teddy were leading the charge, curiosity turned to popularity. Everyone wanted to meet the trio who had chewed, cried, comforted, and conquered. Mum was after all a daily blogger to the group about all their antics and adventures.

Each walk was a parade of wagging tails, humans laughing, muddy paws, and an occasional half-eaten snack stolen from someone's pocket, normally by Bailey.

New friendships forged on woodland trails and in grassy fields.

Lexie, who once walked quietly with Ted and puppy Bill, now found herself at the centre of a furry whirlwind, her heart full, surrounded by kindred spirits and dogs dressed in their finest jumpers.

The Turd Head Walks started small, just a few Cavachon's and their slightly frazzled owners. But as word spread, so did the madness.

First came Princess Poppy. With her mum, dad and human sister, Nora. Poppy was a Princess by name but certainly not by nature. Bill, naturally, fell in love immediately. He tried showing her his favourite bin lid on walk one. She was unimpressed.

Then came Jake, a gorgeous, lovable rogue who galloped through life like he had been caffeinated at birth. He barked at leaves, dug holes just to roll in them, and treated every walk like a full-scale jungle expedition. Joined with his mum. Bailey found his soulmate in Jake, they were zoomie brothers from day one.

Gus, the quiet observer. Gentle eyes, calm energy, long legs and the only one who actually came when called, joined with his mum. He became Teddy's walking buddy, the calm to his cautious, the friend who never rushed him but always waited.

Oscar, a gentle, beautiful soul, who had travelled for miles with his mum and dad. Bailey obviously took a particular liking too Oscar. He was a very handsome boy and Bailey knew it.

More joined, Hector, Bill's brother and litter mate, joined with his brother Merlin, and their dads.

Lexi, a beautiful, super excited ball of fluff, joined with her mum and dad.

Cassie, the smallest of the group shy, at first. She just wanted to be carried by her human sister or dad a little ball of healing power for her family.

Everyone came, each, with their own reasons and, each with their own story.

Together, they formed the extended cast of the Turd Head Universe. Every walk became a rolling, barking, biscuit-fuelled parade of personalities. Lexie couldn't believe her luck. So many fluffy friends, so much love, and absolute, glorious chaos.

And at the heart of it all? Bill, leading the pack, muddy and proud.

Bailey, stealing any food he could from walkers' pockets.

Teddy, wagging slowly beside Gus.

Jake rolling in anything disgusting he could find.

And Princess Poppy, floating through it all like royalty, covered in God knows what.

The Turd Head Trio weren't just mischief-makers anymore. They were local heroes. Facebook famous. Lexie? She was in heaven. Mum, even more.

Lexie had been telling her school friends, Daisy and Alice, all about the "Turd head walks," the chaos, the mayhem, the magic. So obviously they wanted to experience it for themselves. Lexie and Mum were more than willing to oblige. Daisy and Alice were kind, funny, understanding of Lexie and most importantly, completely unfazed by the frenzy that came with three Cavachons. They were used to it from coming to Lexie and the boy's home. Where their socks went missing, biscuits left unguarded were not safe, and laughter guaranteed.

The first time Daisy and Alice joined a "Turd Head Walk" they were warned, "They're a bit wild," Mum had said. But the girls didn't just survive the experience, they loved it. Soon, they were regulars, dodging protest pees, chasing after Bailey, helping Teddy gain confidence, and laughing as Bill did Bill things.

With every walk, the bond between Lexie, Daisy and Alice grew stronger. And so did their connection with the boys.

What started as a dog walk, became a highlight, a joyful, muddy, tail-wagging tradition, filled with chatter, ruckus, and the kind of friendship that sticks, just like paw prints on a clean kitchen floor.

Picnic Pinchers

One sunny afternoon, the Turd Head Trio were on another Cavachon "Turd Head Walk" with their pals, Princess Poppy, Bobby, Bunty, Jake, Gus, Oscar, and the rest of the fluff gang.

The humans had planned a relaxing picnic: blankets, benches, snacks, cold drinks, and the naïve belief that they could eat in peace.

Enter the Picnic Pinchers!

Whilst the "Turd Head Walks" are always a highly anticipated, exciting day out. It soon became apparent that it also came with some difficulties.

Picnics! Picnics, it turns out are the "Turd Head Trio's" favourite pastime.

Bailey always moved first. He moved with stealth, like a creamy fluff ninja, and swiped a cocktail sausage without breaking stride.

Bill would follow with a bold, shameless grab, a whole sandwich, gone in one gulp.

Teddy, still the quiet one, would hover at the edge of the "arena" ... until he spots crisps. One paw, one nudge, and crunch - mission success.

Every "Turd Head Walk" mums/dads/siblings know that when the picnics came out, they become a logistical nightmare.

Owners huddled around food like bodyguards. Blankets surrounded like dog-friendly barricades. Some resort to standing while eating, others give up entirely and just pack extra snacks for the dogs.

Jake's mum even makes the "Turd Head Trio" and their fellow fluffy friends their very own doggy tray bake.

The Trio have become known far and wide as: not just The Turd Heads but also **The Picnic Pinchers**. Their legend grows. Their belly sizes do, too.

And yet, every walk ends the same way: full dogs, laughing humans, and at least one person shouting,

"WHO TOOK MY SAUSAGE?!"

Lexie smiles, laughs, and shrugs.

She always knows exactly who it is.

THE TURD HEAD BIRTHDAY WALK.

Mum had asked Lexie what she wanted to do for her birthday.

Mum expected something simple like a cake at home, Lexie paused, then said firmly, "A Cavachon walk."

Mum smiled. "So… a Turd Head Walk then?"

Lexie crossed her arms. "A Cavachon walk." Lexie never liked the "Turd Head Walk" name. It was demeaning to HER boys.

Fair enough. Officially rebranded: Lexie's Birthday Cavachon Celebration Walk (unofficially still called the Turd Head Walk by everyone else).

Lexie had never been one for parties. Big events. Too much talking. Too much socialising. Too loud. Too many people. Too much everything

But this? Her, her boys, and dogs, lots of dogs. It was the perfect plan.

Invites were sent. Treats were packed. Jumpers for the boys, Lexie and Mum were ordered.

Then… STORM DARRAGH hit. Trees down. Roads blocked.

Mum panicked. She sent out a message:

"Please stay home, stay safe - we'll rearrange."

But the replies flooded in:

"It is Lexie's birthday. If we can get there, we will." And they did.

Poppy arrived first, bounding through the mud like a pig in a puddle. Followed by Nora wrapped up like an arctic explorer. As always, they arrived before Mum, Dad, Lexie, and the boys. "The Boys' Mum" was ALWAYS late.

Bobby came skidding in with his mum, Bunty trotted along beside her mum.

Oscar and his mum and dad forged through blocked roads and wind. Despite the storm they had travelled almost an hour and a half to get there.

Jake couldn't make it - tree across the road, but sent socks with Bill's face printed on them, along with love and a note that read: "You've ruined socks for us forever." Love Jake + mum."

Gus's mum messaged to say they were sad to miss it but were there in spirit and probably covered in tree sap.

The walk was more of a clamber. Trees had fallen across paths. At one point, Mum had to climb over one like some sort of middle-aged ninja warrior. Poppy's dad bounced the tree for extra carnage.

Teddy screamed in horror. His Oscar winning "Mum is dying" scream.

Bill got distracted and wandered off into the undergrowth.

Bailey got distracted and wandered off into someone's open treat pouch.

Lexie? Lexie was beaming. Absolutely in her element.

The café was shut. No problem. Mum and Dad pulled out an extra-large thermos, paper cups, and a slightly squashed birthday cake. Poppy's mum, straight on it without being asked, serving teas, coffee, hot chocolate. Dad quietly cut the cake with a knife he had found from God knows where.

They stood in a circle, wind howling, dogs barking (well Teddy howling) coats flapping and sang "Happy Birthday" to Lexie in the middle of a storm, surrounded by their fur family.

Mum blinked back tears.

Lexie, never said much in way of appreciation, but Mum and Dad could see the joy and warmth in her eyes it was "her best birthday ever", what she wanted, and they all came.

Dad agreed. It was absolutely perfect. Even if his boots were full of water and someone (probably Bill) had eaten half the cake before it was served.

Princess Poppy's Family

Princess Poppy. She maybe Princess by name, but definitely not by nature.

If Poppy saw a puddle, she didn't trot round it but rather dived into it, paws first. She is more likely to be found face-down in a muddy puddle than sat primly on a throne.

Her kingdom? The woods, the lakes, the fields, anywhere she could roll, splash, and emerge proudly covered head-to-tail in muck, twigs in her curly floppy ears, and the biggest open-mouthed tongue flopped out smile.

A girl after Bill's own heart.

The bond, between the fur (Poppy, Bill, Bailey and Teddy) and the families (the Mums, the Dads, and Lexie, and Nora) like their adventures, was, chaotic, and full of joy.

One of Mum's favourite memories was a Christmas games night, hosted, incredibly, at Bill, Bailey, and Teddy's house. The house where Mum still hadn't put up the picture frames properly.

The house where Dad repeatedly said "There is no point in getting new carpets with these three. No make that four" looking at Lexie covered along with Bill, Bailey, and Teddy in mud, leaves, and twigs.

The house where the dining table and chairs hadn't been used in years.

The house that was their sanctuary, their home.

Mum and Dad did not host. Mum was better with dogs than dinners and Dad didn't like people anyway. Mum and Dad had never really been "have people over" types. Dogs, yes. Chaos, yes. But real people? NO. There were no placemats, no wine glasses, no matching plates and certainly not enough chairs. But there they were the whole gang, Poppy and her family (Poppy, Mum, Dad and Nora) laughter echoing off the walls, four dogs flopped in every possible chair and lap.

Autumn perched on the stairs wondering what the hell was going on.

Sausages going missing suspiciously quickly.

And Dad, who "didn't like people," happily perched on the coffee table with a cushion under him, chatting away like it was the most normal thing in the world.

Mum relaxed, definitely giddy, face flushed, she looked around this strange, mad little group and smiled. This was their little fur family, bought together by paws, fur, fun, and laughter it was the kind of night that makes your cheeks ache from smiling. Utterly joyous.

After that, something shifted. They began to share more of life together - picnics at the lakes, Mum's favourite walk, where the dogs charged in and out of the water, bums perched on the edge of benches, backpacks and Poppy's dad's "wonder wagon" filled with not just sandwiches but stories, laughter, and real moments.

Poppy's mum, always grounded and wise, had a way of listening that made you feel heard, and a way of speaking that didn't sugar-coat a thing. She told the truth gently but honestly. Poppys Mum did REAL talk. No fluff, no judgement, just honesty and kindness, wrapped in sarcasm and carried in muddy boots. A rare kind of friend.

The same went for Lexie who always found social situations uncomfortable. Not knowing what to expect, how to react, Mum on edge as Lexie had zero filter and Mum never knew what would come out of her mouth but as Poppy's mum always put it "She's only saying what we are all thinking but don't say".

Lexie, who was better and more relaxed with dogs, than the social pressures of a conversation and everything else that came with that. Lexie often felt the weight of social pressures pressing in from all sides. While other kids glide effortlessly through conversations and friendships, for Lexie it can feel more like a performance she didn't audition for. She tries to fit in, to say the right thing (sometimes) but it doesn't come naturally. Too many conversations to listen to at once, too many questions, too many expectations, too many faces all blur into a world that, for Lexie, just feels too fast, too noisy, too much.
With Bill by her side though, and Bailey, Teddy and Poppy leading the charge, Lexie and Nora could walk side

by side, in a silence so warm and easy. No expectations. No pressure to talk. No need to pretend. Just Lexie, being fully herself.

There was no royal court, but with muddy dogs, lakeside laughs, sausage-stealing antics and games at the kitchen table. This was the kind of kingdom where everyone was welcome, and everyone belonged. Even Dad, although he would never admit that aloud.

This was not just friendship. It was something softer, safer. A kind of quiet magic that only appears when you stop trying so hard and just let yourself belong. Brought together in the most surprising and unexpected of ways, four chaotic balls of fluff.

Mini Break Mayhem

Mum had been so excited.

A Cotswolds getaway with Lexie and the boys. Bill, Bailey, and Teddy, was already a mission in itself. But this trip had something extra special, a much needed catch up with the one and only Princess Poppy and her lovely family. Her mum, her dad, and her human sister, Nora.

They were meeting in the picture-postcard village of Bourton-on-the-Water, a place so idyllic it looked like it had been plucked straight out of a jigsaw puzzle box. Stone cottages, crystal-clear water winding through the centre, ducks waddling about like they owned the place. Perfect… until our furry hooligans arrived.

Mum had barely parked the car before bedlam began. The three boys tumbled out, dragging leads and dignity behind them. Tails wagging, noses twitching.

Poppy and family had already arrived. On time as ever. Looking every bit as excited as Lexie, Mum and the boys were.

Bill, absolutely exhilarated to see his beloved friend Poppy. His whole body wiggled with excitement, tail going like a helicopter blade. In his frenzy, looped his lead around Mum's legs, tying her up like a maypole. His eyes darting between Poppy and Nora, didn't know who to greet first, so he spun in excited circles, tangling everyone up even further. Mum now stuck, and teetering, could just about muster, "Bill!", as Poppy stood patiently, Lexie and Nora giggling, waiting for the whirlwind to calm down.

Bailey was in full on "I love you Poppy!" mode. The moment he saw her, he trotted over with the confidence of a dog on a mission. He sniffed her, gave her an enthusiastic lick on the face, tail wagging furiously, and before anyone could intervene, he launched into a dramatic declaration of love by mounting her in front of everyone. Poor Poppy stood frozen, eyes wide, horrified. Mum, still wrapped up by Bills lead looked the other way and sighed. Lexie howled with laughter, and Poppy's dad simply said, "Well that's one way to say hello!"

Teddy, bless him, didn't know whether to be terrified or thrilled. One minute he was yelping with pure excitement, the next he was lying stock still, frozen by nerves, unsure if this new moment was a celebration or panic. His emotions swung like a pendulum. Bark, freeze, wiggle, bark again, utterly overwhelmed. Just when it seemed that all three boys had settled and peace had been restored, Teddy darted forward, tail wagging madly and promptly peed on the wheel of Poppy's dad's "Sky Bus!" Teddy turned, looked at Mum, with a flicker of what seemed like bravery in his eyes, as if to say, "Ok, I've got this, I'm ready now, I think!"

And the days adventures began.

Poppy's dad had bought their pull along picnic trolley, "the wonder wagon," containing everything they could possibly need. Blankets, chairs, food, drinks, umbrellas.

They managed a stroll through the village, with Lexie walking in contented silence, beside Nora, both holding onto one enormous bag of dog treats like it was a sacred artefact. The dogs tangled themselves into one massive knot more times than Mum could count. Photos were taken, laughter was shared, picnics were eaten in the rain; it was a chaotic but truly fabulous day. When exhaustion hit, somehow, they made it to the riverside green.

Now, in theory, this was the moment of calm. The rest time.

Poppy's mum took Lexie and Nora to the sweet shop, a quaint little treasure trove of sugary delights. Poppy's dad stayed behind with mum and the boys. Finally, Mum sat down with a sigh that carried the weight of three tangled leads and a morning of shouting.

"LEAVE IT!"

"NO!"

"STOP!"

The river burbled peacefully. Tourists strolled by. People smiled and laughed at the dogs.

Bailey began to sniff the air.

Mum did not notice at first, but something shifted.
Bailey stood up straighter. His nostrils flared like a bloodhound on a mission. Then came the glint in his eye.

107

Mum followed his gaze.

Across the green, a man had just unwrapped the most glorious parcel of fish and chips Bourton had likely ever seen. The paper peeled back, steam rose in a dramatic swirl, and the smell hit Bailey's nose like a rocket. Time slowed down.

Bailey leaned forward. His back legs coiled like springs. His lead began to slide through Mums fingers.

Mum's voice caught in her throat, too late to shout.

And then - WHAM!

Poppy's dad launched. One fluid motion. Like a ninja. Like a man half his age possessed by the spirit of a dog-whispering Olympian. He dived, arm outstretched and snatched the lead just as Bailey's paws left the ground.

Gasps all around. The fish and chip man froze, clutching his lunch to his chest, but thankfully laughed. Other fellow picnickers watched in shocked disbelief at "the dog but also the man" A duck waddled away in disgust.

Bailey landed, safely restrained on the grass, spinning round with an expression of pure betrayal. He huffed. He sulked. He flopped down as if he had chosen to stop all along.

Mum, mouth open, blinked at Poppy's dad. "I've never seen a man move like that," she whispered.

Poppy's dad stood tall, puffing out his chest like a Victorian strongman. His face was flushed, his eyes wide but he looked proud.

The girls returned from the sweet shop, faces sticky with sugar and entirely unaware of the drama.

"Why's everyone staring?" Nora asked.

Lexie shrugged. "Probably because Bailey tried to eat someone's dinner again."

Mum laughed, really laughed. People started clapping.

Not for Bailey. Not for the fish.

For Poppy's dad. For the fish-and-chip-saving hero no one knew they needed.

From that day forward, the story was legend in their household. A tale told over dinner and giggles. The day Bourton-on-the-Water narrowly avoided a Chipocalypse.

And as for Bailey? He still dreams about that fish, you know.

Mincemeat Tray-Gate

Christmas magic. Or at least, it was.

Mum had stayed up late, baking like a contestant on The Great British Bake Off: Festive Meltdown Edition.

Three traybakes: one gooey chocolate; one fluffy Victoria sponge; one questionable, but seasonally appropriate mincemeat. Each cake was cut into perfect little slices and placed into ten beautiful gift boxes. Every teacher on Lexie's list was to receive a festive trio of love, sugar, and presentation perfection.

Mum tucked them all carefully into the fridge and collapsed into bed, flour in her eyebrows, muttering something about, "Mary Berry owes me sleep."

The next morning, Mum packed the boxes neatly into a big carrier bag, ready to transport to school. She left it by the front door.

Then, just a quick toilet break. Forty-five seconds, max.

And in that time... Carnage. A scream from Lexie. A sob. A wail that rattled the Christmas tree.

"THEY'VE EATEN THEM! THEY'VE EATEN ALL THE CAKES!!"

Mum bolted from the bathroom. The bag? Empty. The boxes? Gone. The hallway? A disaster zone of crumbs, cardboard, and guilt. Three dogs sat in the middle of it all.

Bill looked proud.

Bailey looked pleased.

Teddy looked like he wanted to rewind time.

Then Mum remembered: Chocolate is poisonous to dogs. Mincemeat is toxic to dogs. Chocolate. Raisins. Currants. Her face went white.

Lexie started sobbing again. Panic set in. Mum grabbed the car keys. Lexie was dropped (well thrown) into school in a storm of tears.

The boys? Straight to the vet. Mum cried all the way there. The boys were rushed in, weighed, checked, and immediately given injections to make them sick.

The sounds. The smells. The shame.

Bill looked betrayed.

Bailey tried to escape.

Teddy… oh, poor Teddy… he cried with each retch.

Then came the charcoal.

Black, sticky, foul-smelling charcoal. Forced into their mouths to soak up any remaining toxins. Bailey and Teddys white fur? No longer white.

Mum was handed a bottle of charcoal solution with the instructions: "Three times a day, for five days." And given a nice hefty bill. Five days of black drool. Black stains on the floor. Black paw prints on the bedsheets.

Bailey refused it unless it was squirted into his mouth with a meat substitute.

Bill tried to weaponize his against the walls.

Teddy cried through every dose.

Mum didn't cry anymore. She just sighed. Deeply.

Lexie told her teachers, "My dogs are being detoxed. We poisoned them. It was a lot."

That Christmas, there were no traybakes. Just stories. And stains. And three dogs with slightly haunted expressions every time the fridge door opened.

Mum added "mincemeat" to her ingredients that are banned for eternity list. Right under "raisins" and just above "trust". Next year, she vowed, "Vouchers. I am doing vouchers. And a locked fridge." Because memories are lovely. But trauma has a flavour. And in their house, it was now chocolate and mincemeat.

New Year, New Brothers

A much needed "minibreak" was a must after THAT Christmas.

The "Turd Head Trio" were headed on a new year relax and refresh! To Norfolk, no less.

The car was packed, around Teddy, the snacks were prepped, and Lexie had exactly twelve inches of space in the back seat... under three Cavachons.

Teddy, sweet boy Teddy, still cried on the journey, not the entire way, and not because he was uncomfortable. It was something deeper. Mum always had a feeling that despite all the love wrapped around him now, a tiny part of Teddy still worried each time the car started moving. Worried that maybe, this would be the journey where it all ended. That this family, this safety, this love might not be forever after all.

Lexie, hearing his whimpers, reached across the seat and stroked his head, the whole way there. Whispering, "We would never leave you, Teddy. You are ours."

Something about that must have stuck, because once they arrived, the boys were on their absolute best behaviour.

Walks on windswept beaches turned into full-speed ball chases.

Teddy stayed close at first, but by the third day, he was bounding across the sand like he had never known fear. Bill led the charge with seaweed in his beard. Bailey tried to steal a fisherman's glove.

And Teddy ran just to feel the wind.

Evenings were spent exploring seaside towns. While Lexie played in arcades, the boys watched her ears perked, tails wagging, their girl always in sight.

That New Year's Eve, as fireworks cracked over the coastline and the waves rolled in gentle and slow, the family huddled together in the caravan watching their favourite film, well Mum and Lexies favourite film, "Wicked" Lexie practising her "Toss Toss," "Toss, Toss, Leg," whilst the three boys were snoozing across the settee.

They weren't just a pack anymore. They were a team. The new year was off to a very furry, very loving start.

The Picnic Pinchers (Total Carnage: Curry Edition)

Back from a lovely relaxing New Years break.

It was a clear, sunny day. Birds chirping.

Lexie playing football in the garden as usual, with Bill as her goalie.

Bailey bounding after the ball.

Teddy running towards the ball. Then thinking better of it and squealing in the opposite direction like he had seen a ghost.

Mum relaxed, for once.

"NEW YEAR, NEW ADVENTURE, BOYS."

What could go wrong?

Answer: a full Indian takeaway, on a picnic blanket, halfway up a hill. Owned by strangers. Unattended for two seconds. Game on.

Before anyone could blink, Bill caught the scent. His tail shot up like a radar, eyes locked.

"Bill, no," Mum said. He went.

"Bailey, don't you...!" Mum didn't even finish her sentence, he followed.

"TEDDY, STAY HERE." Teddy paused… and even he then galloped.

From the bottom of the hill, Mum screamed,

"NO! BILL! STOP!"

"TEDDY, LEAVE IT!"

"BAILEY GET OFF THE RICE!"

Up the hill they soared, the Turd Head Cavalry.

Racing toward their target like heroes in a slow-motion action film, except instead of saving lives, they were about to ruin someone's lunch.

The innocent family, cheerful, kind, freshly unpacking their feast, had no idea what was coming.

First Contact:

Bailey launched straight into the rice like it was a soft bed designed for his belly. He rolled. He wiggled. He ate some.

Bill grabbed a naan the size of a steering wheel and legged it like a dog-shaped pizza delivery man.

Teddy, to Mum's exasperation, now fully involved, charged through a container of tikka masala, skidded on a

116

rogue samosa, and flopped into a pile of poppadoms like he had been training for this moment his entire life.

Lexie stood halfway up the hill, frozen.

Mum screamed.

Dad walked in the opposite direction pretending he did not know any of them.

The family gasped. The curry was airborne.

One teenage boy dropped his phone to try and rescue a pakora.

A poor lady squealed as Bailey licked the chutney off her paper plate.

Bill circled the perimeter, naan in mouth, like a victory lap.

Teddy sat (actually sat) in the middle of it all, tikka on his fur, grinning like a golden retriever who had just solved world peace.

Mum arrived panting, sweating, apologising through gritted teeth.

"I am so, so sorry, they've never - okay, yes they have done this before."

"I... BAILEY, DROP IT!"

The family, to their credit, were somewhere between horrified and hysterical. One woman muttered, "That was the last samosa." Another simply whispered, "Why…?"

The hill was now a warzone of spices and shame. Lexie just stood there, naan on her shoe, eyes wide.

Bill, Bailey, and Teddy sat in a row, tails wagging, lips orange, tongues hanging out in total satisfaction.

The rest stared in pure disbelief.

It was the lowest moment of Mum's public dog-walking career.

It was also the proudest moment of Bill's.

As they left the hill,

Bill smug,

Bailey stained yellow,

and Teddy literally radiating korma.

Mum vowed never to show her face in that place again.

Lexie patted the boys on the head and just said, "ICONIC".

Dad was later found hiding behind a tree.

The legend of The Picnic Pinchers reached mythological status.

From that day on, any hill, any picnic, and especially any whiff of curry…

The Turd Head Trio were on full alert.

The Crazy Cheese Lady

There comes a point in every dog mum's life where dignity just… gives up.

"Cheese" was not just a recall word, it became a lifestyle.

It started with innocent intentions: Just a desperate Mum, a few cubes of cheddar, and three fluffy bandits on the loose. But once it worked, once all three came sprinting back like they were in a dairy-based Olympic event, there was no going back.

For Bill, Bailey, and Teddy's mum, that point arrived somewhere between their third sprint in the opposite direction and the fourth time she was left shouting their names while they pretended to be deaf.

No recall method worked. Not whistling. Not shouting. Not begging. And absolutely not yelling, "TREAT!" - because they knew that one was optional.

Then, one day, in a moment of pure desperation, she yelled it. Not their names. Not "come". Just one word.

"CHEESE!!!"

All three heads snapped round.

Bill froze mid-zoom.

Bailey skidded to a halt so hard he fell sideways.

Teddy, covered in mud, ran toward her like she was the last person on Earth (with legs made of cheddar).

They returned. Immediately. Tongues out. Eyes wide. Pure dairy-fuelled joy. It worked. It worked.

From that moment on, Mum had a new recall word. And she used it. Loudly. Often. Across fields, in parks, near cafes, during dog walks with strangers. "CHEESE!" she would bellow. Three furry missiles would appear. People would stare.

Someone once clapped. The dogs didn't care. They got cheese.

Lexie didn't care. She got her boys back.

Mum? She now had a reputation. She was no longer just "the one with the three fluffy chaotic dogs." She was known far and wide as:

"The Crazy Cheese Lady."

And honestly? She earned it.

Mum began carrying cheese everywhere. Diced cheddar in coat pockets. Grated mozzarella in sandwich bags. Squirty cheese in the glove box.

Park-goers started to notice. Dog walkers whispered, "There she is… the cheesey one."

The real peak? At a busy Sunday Cavachon "Turd Head Walk", when half the pack went rogue chasing a squirrel, Mum raised one arm to the sky and yelled:

"CHEEEEEEEESE!!"

Three Cavachon's turned on the spot like synchronised swimmers.

They galloped toward her in perfect formation, ears flying, tongues lolling, eyes sparkling with lactose lust. She was nearly knocked over by the stampede.

The "Turd Head" Walkers were in awe, amazed.

From that day forward, it was official.

She wasn't just a dog mum.

She was "The Crazy Cheese Lady," summoner of dogs, destroyer of dignity, and undisputed Queen of Recall.

Bill, Bailey, and Teddy? They couldn't be prouder. They hear the word "cheese" and immediately obey. Unless, of course, there's curry nearby. Then all bets are off.

Agility Bound – The Dream Team

Lexie's love was being active and being outdoors. Sitting was boring, uncomfortable. Active was good.

Whether it was football, rounders, swimming, drums. Turd Head Walks ABSOLUETLY.

So when she had an idea, and that idea involved Bill. Her enthusiasm skyrocketed.

At just 11 years old, Lexie had an idea: "I want to do agility training with Bill."

Mum, supportive as ever, set to work. She sent email after email to training groups, but the replies were always the same:

"Sorry, Lexie's too young."

"She wouldn't have the control she needs."

"She's just a child."

Mum scoffed. Excuse me? Obviously, Mum knew best. Still, the doors kept closing.

Until one day, a single Facebook post changed everything. An agility group "Barkaway Dog Agility", in Worcester, nearly an hour's drive away, was hosting a class.

Worth a shot, Mum thought. She sent one more hopeful message. And this time, the reply came back bright and open-hearted: "Of course. We would love to meet them."

Lexie was buzzing. Bill, though entirely unaware of what was coming, bounced around the house with excitement anyway.

The day of their first class, Mum loaded everyone into the car and made the long drive.

When they arrived, Mum went and introduced herself to Bill and Lexie's new instructor Heather.

Lexie turned to her Mum. Eyes serious. "Stay in the car. I need to do this with Bill. Just me and him."

Mum blinked. Oh. But she understood.

From that day on, it became their weekly ritual. Mum sitting quietly in the car, tea in hand, peeking through the windows.

Bill always over excited to see his dog friend Lexi from the "Turd Head Walks" were also at the group with her mum and dad.

Lexie and Bill, out in the field, learning, failing, trying again.

Bill had moments of brilliance and moments of madness, dashing in the opposite direction, trying to say hello to every other dog, mistaking the A-frame for a personal mountain-top. But week after week, something magical began to happen.

Lexie and Bill moved more like a team. The distractions became fewer. The focus sharper. The trust deeper.

The other adults in the group were captivated, not just by Lexie's determination, but by the unspoken connection she had with her dog. A quiet understanding that did not need explaining.

Then one evening, Heather approached Mum in the car. "I think they're ready for their first competition." Mum beamed.

Lexie was less convinced. "What if Bill isn't ready?" she asked, eyes down.

Heather smiled gently. "Just go. Have fun together."

Competition day.

Mum, as instructed, stayed at the edge of the field. Bill, of course, did Bill things.

First run? A classic Bill performance.

He ran halfway through the course before veering off to greet a spaniel, his adoring fans and ooh he was sure he could smell a picnic.

Mum didn't flinch.

Lexie stood her ground.

Heather stepped in, calmly walked to the field, and looked at Bill. "No, Bill. Listen."

Second run. Everything changed.

Lexie breathed in.

Bill looked up. The whistle blew.

And suddenly, Bill was on fire. Every jump, every tunnel, up and down the A frame, up over and down the dog walk, he nailed them all.

The crowd clapped and cheered. Lexie, as ever, stayed humble. A quiet pat on the head for Bill. "Good boy, Bill."

Mum watched, tears filling her eyes. Not just because of the agility. But because of Lexie's quiet power. Her strength. Her bond with Bill. How the world had said, "no," but Lexie had walked into it and said, "Watch me."

They came home with three rosettes: 2nd Place; 3rd Place; Most Improved

But none of those mattered as much as the moment they crossed the finish line, side by side. And, in that moment, Mum knew: They were already champions.

Bill – Who Would Have Believed it!

At home, Bill was still mischievous.

He still rooted through Lexie's school bag, left the odd protest pee, stole pizza, ate Lexie's homework (Mum had to email Lexies school teacher one day to say, "the dog ate Lexies homework"), but beneath the chaos, Bill had a deeper purpose, one only he seemed to understand.

He was Lexie's therapy dog.

The world did not always make sense to Lexie. Sometimes it moved too fast. Sometimes it felt too loud. Sometimes people said things they did not mean, or did not say things they should have, and it all tangled together in her head like a drawer full of knotted string.

But Bill never tangled anything. He understood. He did not ask questions. He did not interrupt. He did not need to know why she was upset, he just was there. When Lexie needed space, Bill gave it. When she needed pressure, he curled against her like a warm, weighted blanket.

When she needed to talk, he listened with those big eyes, that soft stillness, and that slow tail wag that said, "I've got you." She told him everything. Her fears. Her secrets. The feelings she did not know how to explain to anyone else. The things that sat heavy in her heart, the victories that felt too small to share, the thoughts that looped and looped and would not let go. To everyone else, it might have looked like a girl whispering to a dog, but Lexie knew the truth. Bill was her safe place. Her diary. Her calm.

He did not just listen he understood without needing to understand. He was soft fur against her cheek when the world felt sharp. A solid presence when everything else wobbled. And the keeper of every quiet truth she carried. There were no wrong words with Bill. No expectations. Just pure, unfiltered, loyal love.

And in a confusing world that sometimes made her feel lost, Bill was the thing that reminded her: She was never alone.

From the very beginning, Bill had been drawn to her. He didn't just follow her around, he watched her. He listened. He knew. If Lexie was tired or sad, Bill was there curling up beside her, head gently placed on her lap, eyes soft and steady.

If she was anxious, he pressed himself into her side like a furry shield.

If she cried, he did not flinch, he licked her tears and stayed still until the storm passed.

And if she needed a reason to smile, he would do that thing, the thing where he rolled upside down with his legs in the air, tongue out, looking ridiculous, just to make her laugh. Bill did not need training for this. No one taught him how to love so fiercely. He just knew.

While Bailey bounced through life like a small, happy hurricane.

Teddy, dear Teddy, was still trying his best, every day. It was as though Teddy was constantly in a battle with himself. When Mum looked into his eyes, she knew what he was thinking, "I'm ok, I'm loved, I'm safe." But Mum could tell from his small flinches, when someone got too close, or he saw his lead come out, exactly what he was thinking (was the lead out for a walk or was it for something else). Mum knew Teddy still struggled to believe, he was ok, he was loved deeply, and that he was safe.

Bill was Lexie's constant. Her calming anchor in the madness of growing up. He was her snuggle partner on tough days. Her protector when the world felt too loud. Her comfort when words were not enough.

He could be wild. He could be cheeky. But when Lexie needed him, Bill was still. And in that stillness, she always found peace. Everyone already knew it, - Bill was Lexie's dog. Her shadow. Her comfort. Her chaos. Her calm.

When Mum had the great idea of training Bill to officially become a "therapy dog" it felt right. He already knew how to sense Lexie's mood. Already curled up beside her when her world felt too loud. Already loved her in that deep, instinctive way no one had to teach. So, they signed him up for his therapy assessment with big hopes and bigger hearts.

Bill… was enthusiastic. Very enthusiastic.

He walked into the assessment and immediately stole a biscuit from a side table. **FAIL.**

He jumped up to greet the assessor. **FAIL.**
He licked everyone. **FAIL.**

He rolled on the floor. **FAIL.**

He tried to play with a cushion. **FAIL.**

When told to "sit," he stood. **FAIL.**

When told to "stay," he wandered over to see if someone else had snacks. **FAIL.**

When told to "focus," he blinked with love and zero comprehension. Mum half-laughed, half-apologised. The assessor smiled gently and said, "Lovely temperament just a little over enthusiastic."

Bill had **FAILED EVERYTHING** that, as a therapy dog, he was supposed to do.

But then hope came from an unexpected place. One day during a quiet honest chat with Lexie's therapist, a new suggestion was made. "Why not train Bill to be Lexie's ASSISTANCE dog?"

Mum blinked, not wanting to get her hopes up. "How? that takes years of training."

Lexies therapist said, "Look into it, Lexie could train him herself, with the bond they have it shouldn't be too difficult. Lexie and Bill just need to be monitored, assessed together, and signed off by a professional."

Mum was almost bursting. The questions already flooding her weary head "Where do we to do that? Who will we get to monitor them? Assess them? Lexie doesn't engage well with new people, as it is, it takes time and understanding."

The therapist smiled "I will. Bill can join Lexie in her sessions every week, I will watch them, monitor them, assess them without Lexie knowing and if she truly needs Bill with her to live her best life, I can draft a report in agreement."

A new mission began.

There were no fancy classes. No clicker sessions. No obedience medals.

Lexie trained Bill herself. Side by side, day by day, they tackled the world together.

On the train, she taught him to sit quietly at her feet. In shops, she showed him how to focus when the lights and noise got overwhelming. In supermarkets, he learned to stay calm by the trolleys, never leaving her side. Restaurants, which Lexie hated going to anyway, she now asked to go, these became practice grounds for patience, and trying new foods, trying various places because Bill was by her side. The cinema taught him stillness. Bill passed staying still silent, tail wagging softly under her chair the whole time. Lexie guided him with gentle words, quiet reassurance, and treats in her pocket (and occasionally, her sleeve).

And Bill listened.

Not because he had to. Because it was her. He learned to look back at her in busy crowds. To lie against her legs when she needed grounding. To sense when the world became too loud, too fast, too much, and simply be there.

He never wore a perfect vest. He did not always behave like the dogs in training videos, but he never let her down. Lexie did not just teach Bill how to support her, she showed him that he already was. And together, without fanfare or certificates, they built something stronger than any class could promise, - Trust, understanding, and unconditional love.

They did it. After months and months of training, on trains, in shops, at the cinema, under restaurant tables, in lifts, through crowds. Lexie and Bill had become a real team. No classes. No trainers. Just the two of them, figuring it out together. Mum keeping a short, quiet distance behind them.

Every week Bill dutifully attended Lexie's therapy sessions with her. Mum and the therapist noticed she was calmer, more focused, opened up more, she was more relaxed, more regulated. With her hand on Bill's head and Bills paw on her. Lexie began to talk … to Bill.

And then one day, it arrived:
Bill's official Assistance Dog ID card. And with it… His coat. His working coat. His black working coat, sleek, smart, and stitched with bold red writing that read exactly what Lexie already knew:

ASSISTANCE DOG.

Lexie clipped it on with a proud smile. Mum wiped away a tear. Bill stood tall.

Then the real test. The first full day out: Bill in his new ASSISTANCE DOG COAT, ID card in Lexies bag.

A day at The Sea Life Centre, complete with trains, crowds, noisy tunnels, and Lexie had bought her friend Daisy along for the ride. Mum, as always, following silently behind.

On the platform, Lexie stood quietly, gripping Bill's lead with one hand and fidgeting with her sleeve in the other. Lexie noticing every noise, every movement. But Bill stood calm beside her, tail tapping gently, eyes steady and focused, never leaving her. The rumble of the train grew louder. Bill did not budge. He pressed his warm body gently against her leg. She sank down, burying her face in his soft curls. Just breathing. Just anchoring. Then, clear as day, she whispered, "Come on, Bill. Let's go." And just like that, she moved. Instead of freezing, instead of locking down with panic, as she has before, Lexie found the words and Bill gave her the safety to say them. He gave her a way out, a way through.

The train doors whooshed open, and Bill stepped forward, leading her to a quiet seat window side, facing forward. He knew. Somehow, he always knew. While the world bustled around them, Bill lay at Lexies feet like a knight under orders, guarding her.

Inside the Sea Life Centre, the air changed, louder, brighter, unpredictable. Lexie hesitated in the entry tunnel. The shifting lights and echoing voices already threatening to overwhelm her. Mum watched her scratching at her arms, her breath start to catch. Bill nudged her, once, twice. Lexie dropped her hand onto his head without thinking. Then, brave as anything, she said again, "Come on, Bill. It's too busy here, isn't it?" They stepped to the side, away from the bottleneck of people, and waited together. People walked past, some smiling gently at the sight of the two of them. Others stepped aside slightly, giving them space. Bill never once took his eyes off her. He stayed close, alert, a calm presence in the turbulence. In his vest, his "coat of armour", just for her. He stood like a little soldier, guarding his girl. Through tanks of glowing jellyfish and past the playful otters, Lexie found her feet again. She laughed, pointed things out, chatted to Bill like he was her tour guide. With other poor parents with their own screaming children, Lexie just looked at Bill, and whispered, "It's very noisy isn't it? Let's go" and onwards they went.

Bill was fascinated by the penguins swimming below him in the water, but never once barked (like he does at a squirrel, sometimes another dog) Bill was in "work mode, there for Lexie and Lexie only".

After the hustle and bustle of the Sea Life Centre Mum and Lexie's friend Daisy needed a pause, a sit down, and lunch. Lexie thought the concept of stopping life to eat was ridiculous, but Mum insisted Bill needed a rest and some lunch as well, so despite the rain they found a covered spot at the nearby conference centre for their indoor picnic.

The security man eyed them as they should, looking at Bill. "Can he come in?"

"He's my Assistance dog," Lexie said before Mum could speak, Lexie's voice sure and steady.

"Of course," as he smiled. "He's doing a brilliant job."

Bill curled under the table without a fuss. He did not beg. He did not even sniff the picnic. He just kept his eyes on Lexie, quietly watching. Bill got his lunch of cucumber, chicken, and the odd crisp under the table by Lexie, Daisy, and Mum.

On the train ride home, Lexie's hand rested on Bill's head as he dozed off. A group sat next to them laughed as they suddenly noticed Bill fast asleep on Lexie's lap 15 minutes into their journey home. "I didn't even realise there was a dog there". Lexie smiled and stroked Bill's head. Mum found herself again, blinking back tears. This dog, this cheeky, mischievous whirlwind of chaos, had become her daughter's shield. Her confidence. Lexie's way to say, "I'm not okay," without needing to explain why.

Bill was not just a dog anymore. He was Lexie calm in the storm. For the first time, people stopped and noticed. "He's so calm."

"What a good dog."

"Wow, he's amazing."

And he was.

When that coat was on, he was focused, quiet, collected. Lexie and Bill were unstoppable. Shops? Easy. Crowds? No problem. Public transport? Piece of cake (as long as no one dropped one). He became more than her best friend. He was her anchor in public, her confidence in unfamiliar places, her safety net when things felt shaky. All wrapped up in fluff and love and a shiny ID card.

When they got home it was a different story. The coat came off and that was when mayhem resumed. The second that coat came off and dropped to the floor, Bill's tail shot up like a rocket. He bounced. He barked. He zoomed. It became a routine:

Coat on? Serious. Coat off? Turd Head activated.

Lexie laughed every time. Looking into his eyes with such love, pride, and trust. That is what made him perfect. He could be calm. He could be focused. He could be her support, her strength, her brave partner in a complicated world.

But when the coat came off? He was just Bill. Lexie's wild, ridiculous, one-of-a-kind best friend. And honestly, she would not change a single thing.

Now? Taking Bill out as Lexie's assistance dog always fills Mum with quiet pride. No matter where they go whether it is the noisy platforms of the train station, the echoey halls of the Sea Life Centre, or a bustling restaurant, Bill is right there, focused, loyal, calm. His tail gives a little wag whenever Lex reaches down to touch him. It is as if he understands this is his job, and he would not let her down.

He always puts Lexie first. If someone (usually a child) reaches to pet him, he will lean closer to her instead. If she pauses, unsure of her surroundings, Bill stops too, solid and steady. When the lights get too bright or the noise too loud, he will nudge her gently, anchoring her. To the world, he might look like just a dog, but to Lexie, he is a best friend, a guide, a reason to feel safe.

And Mum, watches them together, he is a little miracle in fur. On quiet walks, shops, even coffee stops with Bill proudly wearing his assistant dog vest.

And when people ask, "Does Lexie really need Bill with her?" and they do ask!

They do not deserve an answer.

Tapas, Tails, and the Great Jacuzzi Bed

There is something magical about going to lunch at a friend's house, especially when that friend is Princess Poppy. Her house was like stepping into a warm hug: twinkly fairy lights in the garden, beautiful bowls of food laid out like a banquet, and a constant chorus of giggles, barks, and clinking glasses.

It was a sunny weekend when the invitation arrived: "Come for lunch! Bring the boys!" And of course, Mum said yes. Even when mentioning to Dad, "We've been invited over for lunch," Dad stilled, placed his cup down took a deep breath and said "Who's" "Poppys," Mum replied. Dad breathed out a sigh of relief. Although they all knew there would be at least some level of mischief involved, because bringing Bill, Bailey, and Teddy to lunch is never just lunch. It is an event.

They arrived like a small, furry hurricane. Poppy greeted them at the door with all the poise of a princess, tail wagging in polite delight. Nora immediately going in for the hug, which Mum embraced as always. Lexie smiled and raised her fist, Lexie does not do hugs. A knowing fist bump, a gentler smile, a quiet understanding between them all. The girls raced off down the garden, dogs in tow already halfway through choosing who would be on Lexie's team for hide and seek. Poppy's mum had gone all out - tapas-style.

Bowls of olives, warm breads, marinated peppers, chorizo, cheese, dips that looked too pretty to touch - and Mum, well, her eyes lit up like a Christmas tree.

Everyone gathered around the garden table, stories flowing like the wine and Pimm's, sunshine bouncing off wine glasses. Mum was mid-sentence about Lexie and Bills plans for the half term holiday and what assistant dog training he was going to do. When,

CRASH.

Bill had sprinted down the garden like he had just remembered he left the oven on. Closely followed by a bouncing Bailey and Teddy yelping no idea what was going on. Lola, Poppy's long-suffering family cat, had made the fatal error of moving ever so slightly from her nap spot on the windowsill. Bill took it as a personal invitation to play.

A hiss was heard, a bark a yelp a "Boys Jeysus Christ, stop it," Lola flew across the garden like a streak of grey lightning.

Bailey barked in excitement. Poppy barked in protest. Teddy stood in the doorway, watching the madness unfold, head cocked thoughtfully like, "Hmm, maybe chaos is my brand too."

By the time the adults had retrieved the dog squad, half the tapas had been nudged, jostled, or enthusiastically sniffed. Bill had dipped his ear in the olive oil. Bailey had attempted to run off with a breadstick. And Teddy?

Teddy had disappeared.

The hunt began. Upstairs, downstairs, garden shed, no sign. Eventually, Nora spotted him: curled up on top of the jacuzzi cover, snoring softly, his little snores bouncing off the plastic shell like a soothing spa soundtrack.

Mum nearly cried laughing.

The boys Dad just shook his head and muttered something about needing a holiday. Poppy's mum, to her eternal credit, simply refilled the wine glasses and said, "Well, it's not a real lunch without a bit of drama."

The afternoon rolled on with sun, snacks, and giggles. Lola emerged eventually, tail twitching in disdain, and claimed the one shaded chair like a queen reclaiming her throne.

Bill launched again! Followed by more mutterings from Dad, Mum and Lexie retrieved them all. Leads put on and they slowly settled. Teddy on the jacuzzi. Bailey under the table with a napkin, Bill pretending to be innocent beside Nora.

When it was finally time to leave, Mum repeatedly saying, "Oh this has really been the Best Day Ever."

Lexie rolled her eyes as this seemed to be something Mum always said, especially after spending a day with Poppy and her family, offered Nora her fist again. Nora giggled and bumped it right back, no words needed.

As they piled into the car, Mum sighed, sun and Pimm's kissed, full of tapas, slightly mortified, but happy.

And, as for Poppy's family? It was just another normal visit with the boys, bedlam, fun and laughter.

The type they had all learnt to love and expect.

But from that day on, whenever someone mentioned "a casual lunch," everyone would pause, glance at the jacuzzi, and quietly wonder… where would Teddy nap this time?

Sideline Supporters

From the very first kick of the season, the boys were there. Bill, Bailey, and Teddy. Just like Ted and Bill had been seasons before. Lexie's very own unofficial/official football supporters.

They were not technically on the team list. They were not always exactly "welcome" by the referees. But they were there. Every match they were allowed to attend, they showed up in style. And noise.

Bill took his role very seriously, sitting as close to the touchline as humanly (or doggedly) possible. Eyes locked on Lexie with a deep sense of confusion. "Why is she chasing the ball and I'm not? I'm clearly the more qualified candidate." Occasionally, a low whine would escape him, a protest bark when she got too far from his line of sight.

Bailey, ever the opportunist, was less focused on the game and more on the crowd. He had perfected the art of the "please feed me" stare. If you were holding a bacon or sausage sandwich, you were absolutely his new best friend. Bonus points if you dropped something. You would never beat him to it.

Teddy, bless him, had only one goal. Do not let Mum leave his sight. If she dared step even one pace away, perhaps to get a coffee, or speak to another teammate's mum. Teddy would let out an Oscar-worthy wail. A high-pitched, theatrical, "My world is ending!" sort of scream.

Parents turned, kids paused mid-pass, the other teams, Lexie's team's parents were used to his theatrical performances and just carried on shouting unwanted advice "Oh that's just Teddy," Mum would say, climbing back into his line of vision.

Over time, Lexie's teammates began to adore them. They became the team's official mascots in everything but name.

In Winter, they arrived in fluffy dinosaur coats. At Halloween, they wore pumpkin jumpers or bat wings. In December, Santa himself appeared to be riding their backs, ho-ho-hoing his way through the mud.

There were laughs. There were photos.

There was Dad muttering behind his coffee cup, "Don't touch that one, he's just rolled in fox poo." Usually Teddy! Sometimes Bailey, often Bill. At some points, all three.

And at the end of every game, win, lose, or draw, Lexie would jog off the pitch, straight into the frenzy of wagging tails and muddy paws. Because no matter the score, she already had her biggest cheerleaders waiting for her.

Her boys. Her team. Her heart.

Protest Pees and Public Humiliation

It started with the infamous bin pee.

Bailey, caught on camera mid-chaos, made direct eye contact with Mum, and lifted his leg on the kitchen bin like he was signing an official complaint. But he did not stop there.

Bailey had discovered something powerful: **the Protest Pee.**

Tell him off? He would wander off slowly… and pee up the chair. No biscuit after walkies? He would casually strut over to the washing basket, or the poor house rabbit, "Bunny's" hutch and leave a little message.

Then came the public protest. At the park, a child left their bright green bike helmet on the ground. Bailey sniffed it. Considered it. Lifted his leg. Lexie screamed. Mum gasped. The child's mum was not amused.

Bailey trotted off smugly. It became a theme.

Picnic tables, plant pots, one poor man's bag on a bench. Bailey's protest pees were unpredictable, swift, and oddly targeted.

And then… Bill joined in.

Not every day. Not while "on duty," but on his off-lead, off-coat, off-duty days. When the mischief returned, Bill got involved.

Mum and Lexie had been going to Dog Fest for years. The first year, Dad had come along with Ted, bless him. But as the quiet, reserved man he was, he had found the entire day, well a bit much. "Too hot. Too noisy. Too many dogs," he had muttered halfway through, clutching his lukewarm tea and giving Mum the please never again look.

So, future Dog Fests were strictly Mum and Lexie affairs. Except now they met the whole fur family. With Jake, Gus, Teddy, Bailey, Bill, and a mountain of dog bags in tow, they arrived bright and early ready for mayhem.

Mum was in her element: So many stalls! So many coats! Toys! Beds! Treats! No Dad there to say, "They don't need another coat." So, of course… they got new coat, new treats, new toys.

Lexie was in heaven, surrounded by her people - dogs and their wonderfully chaotic owners.

Jake impressed everyone with his scent work displays.

Lexie proudly ran Bill through an agility demo.

Gus bounced through it all, wagging his tail like he owned the field.

Then came the competitions. Lexie entered Bill in "Most Handsome Dog." He lost. Shocking!

Mum entered Teddy in "Best Rescue." He didn't even place. Mum looked stunned. Outraged. Ready to write a letter of complaint until the winner was announced: A blind rescue dog from Romania. Both eyes gone, tail still wagging.

Mum nodded with a tear in her eye: "Fair enough. Worthy winner." Teddy? He was just happy he could see Mum. That was all he ever needed.

Lexie entered herself and Bill into "The Best Dog Companion" competition. Through Bill she told the Judge how much he helped her, supported her, loved her. Obviously, they won. As Mum stood outside the arena tears of pride in her eyes.

Next up, a session titled "My Dog Doesn't Listen to Me." And oh, it delivered.

Jake, dressed in his cooling vest, refused to participate, wedging himself under his mum's bag like a furry lump of defiance.

Gus was just happy to be on a day out with his friends to pay full attention, but he did love eating all the treats he was offered to try and get him to listen.

Teddy howled the moment Mum stepped a foot away his trademark howl, "My life has ended, I'm going to die."

Bailey? He was exploring stalls and most definitely not listening.

Lexie stood at the side, arms folded, whispering to Bill, "You don't need this class. You're better than this." Bill looked away, unimpressed. By the end, the trainer simply sighed. Nothing had been learned. Except, maybe, that this group was hopeless but happy.

Then came the "Squirrel Chase Remote-Control Race." The whole crew entered as one furry family. They were chaos in motion.

Jake excelled, chasing the motorised squirrel with Olympic enthusiasm.

Bailey gave it a go but got distracted by someone holding a sandwich.

Gus joined in out of sheer joy.

Teddy? Overwhelmed. He laid down next to Mum, watching only her.

Then Bill... Fed up, unimpressed, and possibly slightly insulted by the whole experience, he wandered off...and lifted his leg and there he did THE PROTEST PEE, right on Gus's mum's bag.

Lexie gasped, "Muuuuum..."

Mum turned just in time to see the protest pee. Too late. Damage done. Bag ruined.

"BILL!" she shouted, but he was already trotting away tail wagging.

Everyone stared. The whole crew burst out laughing. Even Gus's mum waved it off like a badge of honour. "At least he didn't pee on me."

It was a disaster. It was ridiculous. It was Dog Fest.

And somehow, it was absolutely perfect.

Night Falls

"What did we do?" Dad says this most days. He said it when Bill barks, at nothing in particular.

He said it when Bailey zoomed through the kitchen with a slipper in his mouth.

He shouted it when Teddy accidentally set off the 3 a.m. chorus of barking and meowing with one perfectly placed howl in the night.

The noise. The hair. The muddy paws. The smell. The constant, swirling mayhem.

"There's fur in my coffee." "Why is there a sock in the sink?" "WHO TOOK MY PEANUTS?!"

Mum would just smile.

Lexie would giggle.

When the boys have been walked, fed, wiped down (twice), and given their last "you are not hungry, you're just greedy" treats.

The house will settle. The zoomies will slow.

Downstairs, Teddy will wait by the settee, his eyes wide and unsure, like the quiet might mean something is wrong.

Mum will sit and invite him up next to her. Whisper soft things, stroke the place behind his ears where he likes it most. "Good boy," she will say. "You are safe. I am right here." Teddy sighs. And slowly, finally he settles.

Bill will patiently wait at the bottom of the stairs for his command from Lexie. "Ready to receive," his nightly mission already in motion. He will race up the stairs, jump onto Lexie's bed like clockwork. He doesn't need asking. It is his job. Her personal weighted comfort blanket, watching her until her breathing slows and her hands relax. He does not move. He does not sleep. Not until she does.

Bailey will already be flat out. Upside down, legs in the air, tongue out, snoring like a chainsaw. He will dream of sausages, of foxes he will never catch, of "Turd Head Walks" and stealing someone's crisps. His tail will give the occasional twitch, like joy is still bouncing around, even in his sleep.

Dad will settle on the settee with Mum. Bailey, realising Dad has finally sat down, asleep just moments before, suddenly springs to life as if powered by rockets. With a startled yelp of excitement, he waits for no invitation and launches himself on Dad's lap. Stretched out, head on his chest. One second Dad is relaxing, the next he is being smothered by a flurry of white fur, floppy ears, and overwhelming declarations of love. "What is that smell?", Dad will say, as he smiles at his "Bailey bop", and they all relax for the hour that is left of the day.

They would not change a thing.

And after the quiet hour, Mum? She will not go to bed straight away. She will tidy the dog blankets. Check the water bowls. She will walk through the house like she is closing it down gently, one light at a time.

Always making sure one light is left on as "Teddy doesn't like the dark."

Mum cannot sleep until it is quiet. Until all three boys are settled.

Until Bill is watching over Lexie.

Until Teddy is curled and calm.

Until Bailey is snoring like a tractor in a blanket.

Then, and only then, does Mum allow herself to exhale. Because only when they rest, can she rest.

She goes upstairs where Autumn is found meowing on the bed for his treats, which he gets in copious amounts.

Mum crawls under the covers and Winter creeps out from her hiding place, joins Autumn on the bed and slowly slides under Mum's arm pawing for her own quiet time and snuggles with Mum.

And tomorrow?

They will do it all again, barking, biscuits, cuddles, chaos, love. But for now, in the stillness of a house full of dog hair and heartbeats… There is peace.

What we Found Along the Way

People often say, "It's just a dog."

But what they do not see is the muddy pawprints in the hallway of their hearts. The wagging tail that silenced the panic. The gentle nudge in the dead of night that whispered, "I'm here."

It started with Ted.

Ted, who rescued Mum and Dad in the saddest and darkest of times. When dreams had been lost, and everything felt too quiet, too sad, too desperate. He did not come with instructions, just love. And somehow, that was enough. Enough to get Mum back outside into the world again. Enough to make Dad laugh again. Enough to show them they still had space in their hearts for joy.

Then came Lexie a whirlwind of crawling, crying, curiosity. Ted took one look at her and claimed her as his. He was her calm, her anchor, her shadow.

Then came Bill. Wild-eyed, with the most amazing eyebrows, beard-faced Bill. A Tasmanian devil in a dog suit.

Ted tried to teach him how to be a good boy. It did not always go to plan.

When Ted grew old, it was Bill who sat by his bed. Bill who stopped stealing socks (well, briefly). Bill who howled when Ted left. Who did not eat. Who waited. Who grieved.

In that silence, Teddy and Bailey arrived. Not to replace Ted. Never. But as if sent by Ted himself, to bring light back into Bill's world, to remind him that life still had bums to sniff and bins to raid. To give him new brothers, new adventures, new reasons to run.

Bill, once the little brother, now guiding Teddy, a soul so scared he hid behind Mum's legs.

Bailey, sock thief and unbothered menace, quietly becoming the glue.

Together, they did for Bill what Ted once did for Mum and Dad.

Together they bought chaos, mayhem, love and laughter that took them all by surprise.

Somehow, through muddy walks and snoring nights and fox poo disasters, the world opened up. Because these boys, this trio of mischief and magic, brought people together. One wagging tail at a time, they pulled strangers into conversations. Created new friendships. Real ones. Not the polite nod-at-the-park kind. The real kind.

The kind built on laughter, shared eyerolls, muddy boots, and knowing exactly what it means when someone shouts, "CHEESE!" across a field.

Built on early morning mayhem, shared glances, and the universal understanding that, "yes, your dog just did that."

Lexie found her confidence out there. Her people. Her laughter. Her place in the world.

Mum found something too. Not just strength, but community. A fur family.

The boys brought people together. One stolen sandwich, one wagging tail at a time. They created their own community: A little crew of waggy-tailed chaos.

Bunty the flirt. Bobby the rascal. Princess Poppy, not a princess at all. Jake the muck monster. Gus the long-legged gentleman.

People from different places, different stories, all pulled into orbit by the gravitational force of Cavachon Chaos.

It never mattered where anyone came from, just that they all ended up on the same field, with the same bags of treats and the same love in their pockets.

And Lexie? She found friends too. Kind ones. Understanding ones. People who saw her exactly as she was and celebrated her.

These friendships were not planned. They were not perfect. But they were real. And joyful. And exactly what was needed.

There were pub lunches, windy beach days, soaked-through walks, and shared chips.

There were text messages that started as, "Help, my dog just ate…" and ended with, "if it wasn't for the boys we would never have met."

And at the centre of it all: Three fluffy boys, a girl with a huge heart. And the kind of love that ripples outward.

So maybe, it never was just about dogs.

Maybe, it was about what they bring out in people. Kindness. Laughter. Connection. And the reminder that even on the most chaotic days… We are never in it alone.

It may have started with one quiet dog and a lost dream. But it became something bigger than they could have ever imagined.

A life. A family. A tribe built from paws and patience. And so much love.

And while this book might be ending. The walks are not. The chaos is not. The laughter is not. They will still be out there. With the Turd Head Trio. With Lexie, smiling in the wind. With new friends found in the most unexpected places.

And Ted, always. In every soft moment. In every brave step forward. Still leading the way.

157

If you ever come across us, "The Boys, Mum, Dad and Lexie." Whilst we are out and about in the world, it won't be difficult to tell who is who. All the boys come with a distinct warning on their harnesses.

Teddy – NERVOUS RESCUE

Bailey – PICNIC PINCHER - I STEAL FOOD.

Bill – I'M A TURD HEAD (but only when off duty)

So …. Who did rescue who?

The Paws we have Loved and Lost

When you get a dog, you gain more than muddy pawprints, chewed slippers, and a permanent layer of fur on every item of clothing you own. You gain a whole world, a wagging-tailed tribe of people who just get it. The ones who won't bat an eye when your pockets are full of biscuits or you refer to yourself as "Mum" while talking to a four-legged creature in public.

Through the boys, Ted, then Bill, and now Bailey and Teddy, I found my people. The ones who know what it means to love a dog so fiercely they are never "Just a pet." We bonded on dog walks, at parks, in pubs where our dogs caused havoc under the tables and over countless messages and photos of muddy mischief and settee snuggles.

But loving deeply comes at a price. Sometimes, sadly, the group chat falls silent. Walks go ahead with one lead fewer and one of us has to say goodbye.

I've cried with mums I barely know. Just from reading their goodbye posts. I've sat in the car, hugging my Boys', reading about another friend whose heart had broken that morning. I've held onto my Boys' tighter, knowing theirs had taken their final walk.

What I have to remember is, I am so lucky to have known them at all. That I have shared my highs and my lows, with these beautiful furry creatures. Because when the tears come - and they always do, we're not just crying for

159

the loss, we're crying for the joy, the mayhem, the soft heads rested on our laps. The tail wags that said, "You are my whole world."

Some of these friends I've never met in person. Some I've shared cups of tea and tears with on park benches while the dogs wrestled in the mud. And some, I know will be in my life forever, because we've been through the same kind of heartbreak and come out the other side. Not quite whole, but stitched back together with stories, photos, and the understanding nod of someone who knows.

And just when we feel like we will never smile again, along comes another dog, usually naughty, usually needy, always full of love. Not to replace, never that, but to remind us that the love didn't die. It just changed shape.

We might be slightly bonkers, overrun with dog hair and constantly armed with poo bags and tissues, but we are a pack. A beautiful, slightly broken, entirely dog-mad pack.

There's a strength in this strange, wonderful community. We honour the dogs we've lost by loving the next ones. By telling their stories. By laughing again, eventually. At the memories, even the naughty ones. Especially the naughty ones.

Ted will always be part of our story. The gentle start and the hope. To what became utter, joyful madness. He helped shape Bill, who now helps Teddy and that legacy of love continues, with every pawprint that follows.

So, to every friend who's walked this path before me, beside me, or after me; Thank you. Thank you for sharing your dogs with me. Thank you for understanding why I talk to mine like they're tiny hairy humans. Thank you for your compassion, your memories, and your friendship.

To my fellow dog mums and dads who've said goodbye to their best friends; I see you. I hear you. I stand with you. And I carry your stories with mine.

We may lose them, but we never lose the love or their stories.

About the Author.

"The Boys" and Lexie's Mum, is a lifelong animal lover, and enthusiastic storyteller who never imagined her quiet life would turn into a whirlwind of fur, mischief, and muddy pawprints.

With a home full of Cavachon and cat mayhem, and heart, she shares her family's real-life tales of laughter, love, and the occasional stolen sausage.

"The Boys' Mum" still finds time to take Lexie to her extracurricular activities - Drumming lessons, dog agility, football, and swimming, where "The Boys' Mum" is also a swimming teacher.

To relax, Mum enjoys baking for friends, family, and her colleagues. She works with children with complex needs.

Her writing is inspired by her daughter Lexie's bond with her assistance dog Bill, the memory of their beloved Ted, and the joyful madness brought by rescue brothers Bailey and Teddy. When she is not wrangling dogs, the Boys' Mum enjoys walks at the lakes, laughing with friends, and accidentally adopting cats during her lunch break.

This is her first book, written from real life events, that have happened with love, humour, and a lot of dog hair.

Follow their hilarious stories on Instagram @lifeofpetstedbillbaileyteddy

"They may not speak, but they have taught me EVERYTHING I need to hear."